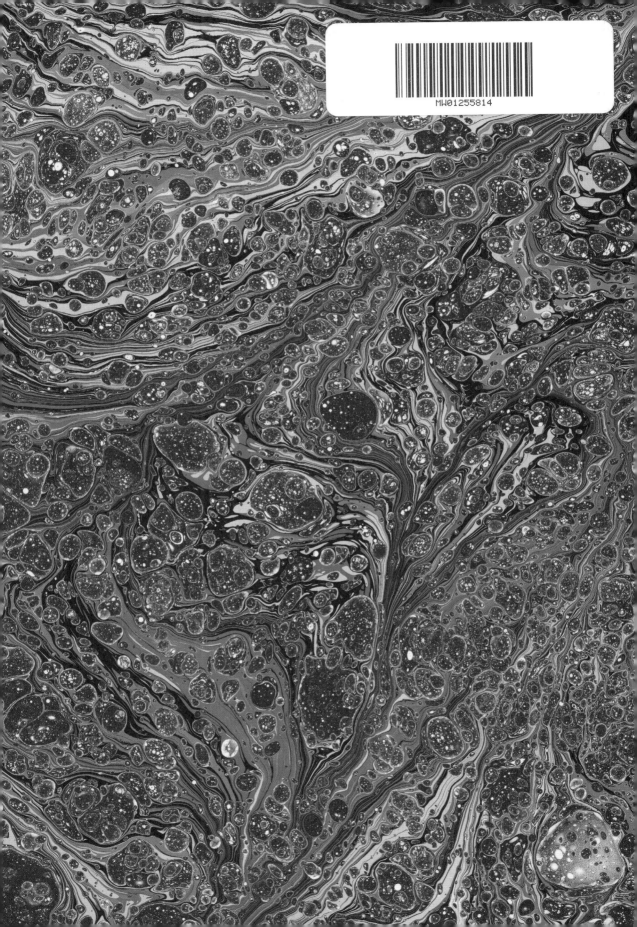

The History of the 24. Waffen-Gebirgs [Karstjäger]-Division der SS
and the Wearers of the Anti-Partisan War Badge in Gold

Rolf Michaelis

Schiffer Publishing Ltd®

4880 Lower Valley Road • Atglen, PA 19310

Bibliography

Bundesarchiv Koblenz, NS 33/108, 113-114
Bundesarchiv Berlin, R 70/Italien

    Baum, Walter/Weichold, Eberhard, *Der Krieg der Achsenm.chte im Mittelmeer-Raum*, Göttingen, 1973.
    Carnier, P.A., *Lo sterminio mancato – La dominazione nazista nel Veneto Ozientale 1943/1945*, Mailand 1982.
    Ferenc, Tone Dr., *Krasoslovec in jamar, polkovnik in zlocinec dr. Hans Brand*, Nove Gorica, 1979.
    — *Dva od njih so obglavili s sekiro. Okupatorjew zlocin v Idrijskih Krnicah*, o.O., 1979.
    Michaelis, *Rolf, Die Chronik der 24. Waffen-Gebirgs[Karstj.ger]-Division der SS*, Erlangen, 1992.
    — *Die Gebirgs-Divisionen der Waffen-SS*, Erlangen, 1994.
    — *Die Waffen-SS: Mythos und Wirklichkeit*, Berlin, 2006.
    Piekalkiewicz, Janusz, *Krieg auf dem Balkan 1940-1945*, München, 1984.
    Schmidt-Richberg, *Der Endkampf auf dem Balkan*, Hiedelberg, 1955.
    Schneider-Bosgard, Hanns Dr., *Bandenkampf in der Operationszone Adriatisches Küstenland*, Triest o.J.
    Schröder, Josef, *Italiens Kriegsaustritt 1943*, Göttingen, 1969.
    Stuhlpfarrer, Karl, *Die Operationszonen "Alpenvorland" und "Adriatisches Küstenland,"* Wien, 1969.

Library of Congress Control Number: 2014946838

Designed by Robert Biondi and Rolf Michaelis
Type set in Georgia/Gill Sans Std

ISBN: 978-0-7643-4802-0
Printed in China

Published by Schiffer Publishing, Ltd.
4880 Lower Valley Road
Atglen, PA 19310
Phone: (610) 593-1777; Fax: (610) 593-2002
E-mail: Info@schifferbooks.com

Translated from the German by David Johnston.

This book was originally published under the title,
Die Träger des Bandenkampfabzeichens in Gold, und der Einsatz der 24.Waffen-Gebirgs [Karstjäger]-Division der SS,
@ 2011 by Michaelis-Verlag, Berlin, Germany.

Contents

Foreword

During the course of the Second World War, the partisan war assumed tremendous dimensions for the German Reich. In 1944, one-million partisans were engaged in battle against the German military all across Europe. Hitler ultimately created the Anti-Partisan War Badge to recognize those who fought against these various resistance movements. The decoration's highest grade, in gold, was first awarded in 1945 and is one of the rarest decorations of the Third Reich.

The purpose of this book is to describe the history of this war badge as well as the units from which the verifiable recipients came. In addition, in cooperation with the Federal Archive and the *Wehrmacht* Information Office in Berlin, I have tried to compile short biographies of the soldiers decorated with the Anti-Partisan War Badge in Gold.

The war against the partisans, dubbed *Bandenkampf* (literally "fight against bandits") at the time, differed greatly from the conventional war at the front, especially with respect to its unusual psychological effects on the soldiers and the great suffering of the civilian populations. The reader may take this into consideration.

I wish to thank all of those who helped in the publication of this book. Special thanks go to Dario Fiorelli, the previously mentioned archives, and to the veterans who generously shared their wartime experiences with me.

Rolf Michaelis
Berlin, November 2011

The War Against the Partisans

During the Second World War the German military was forced to fight a war against partisans in its occupied territories that took on unexpected dimensions as the war progressed. In every country, the guerilas were divided into various groups that always included nationalist and communist elements. In addition to the Germans, they also fought each other with the postwar political order in mind.

In the areas occupied before the summer of 1941, nationalist rebels predominated at first. It was not until the attack on the Soviet Union that communist partisans also began diversionary actions. Significantly, during a meeting at Führer Headquarters on 16 July 1941, Hitler declared:

> *"The Russians have now issued an order for partisan warfare behind the front. This partisan war also has its advantage: it gives us the opportunity to exterminate those who oppose us."*

In fact, the German efforts were not just directed against the partisans actively fighting the German forces, but also against the Jewish population of Eastern Europe, who again and again were targets of reprisals for partisan attacks. In addition to the struggle for political-economic domination in the occupied areas, the guerilas were also directed to occupy as many German forces as possible. German lines of supply to the front were to be interdicted by blowing up railroad lines, roads and bridges and destroying important military installations. Partisan units were particularly active before major Allied offensives. The partisans also tried to prevent German exploitation of labor forces, agricultural products and raw materials. In their attacks on German troops and collaborators, the partisans not only accepted resulting reprisals against the – often innocent – population, but in fact obviously counted on them.

In fact, there developed a dynamic which consisted of action and reaction and which frequently led to brutal events. Although Hitler basically accorded peripheral significance to the struggle against the partisans, sixteen months before the end of the war he created a special decoration for those engaged in the so-called "fight against bandits." The term "fight against bandits" appeared in the autumn of 1942, when Himmler decreed that "partisan," a word idealized in the Soviet Union, should no longer be used. Henceforth the insurgents were to be called "bands" or "bandits."

The Creation of the Anti-Partisan War Badge

O n 29 January 1944, roughly two-and-a-half years after the start of the war behind the front, which later assumed enormous proportions, Hitler created the Anti-Partisan War Badge. The *Wehrmacht* High Command's press office subsequently wrote of this:

> *"The Führer has created the Anti-Partisan War Badge, which is to be awarded to German soldiers engaged against the bands organized by Moscow in the forests and swamps behind the Eastern Front and in the hills and gorges of the mountains of southeastern Europe, or to their brothers in arms from the allied European states, in recognition of their bravery and service."*

The implementing decree of the same day formulated the articles more precisely. Contrary to the press release, the decoration was not associated with any particular regional area of operations and had not been conceived solely for the struggle against Communist partisans:

> 1. *I am creating the Anti-Partisan War Badge in recognition of the actions in the enemy's ever better organized and intensive partisan campaign.*
> 2. *The Anti-Partisan War Badge is a bravery and service decoration. Three grades of the Anti-Partisan War Badge will be awarded (Bronze, Silver and Gold).*
> 3. *The Anti-Partisan War Badge will be worn on the left chest.*
> 4. *Recipients will receive an award certificate.*
> 5. *The Anti-Partisan War Badge will be retained by the surviving dependents of the recipient in the event of his death.*
> 6. *Implementing regulations to be issued by the Reichsführer-SS.*

As the war against the partisans was primarily the mission of the German Police, Hitler left it to Himmler, its commander, to define the further conditions for the awarding of the decoration. Subsequently, on 1 February 1944, Himmler announced:

> 1. *The Anti-Partisan War Badge is a bravery and service decoration.*
> 2. *The Anti-Partisan War Badge will be awarded as recognition for success in the war against bandits. It will be awarded in three grades (bronze, silver, gold).*

3.   *The Anti-Partisan War Badge can be awarded to officers, non-commissioned officers and enlisted men in all German units engaged in the war against bandits.*

4.   *The conditions for awarding of the decoration are:*
a) for the first grade (Bronze) = 20 combat days
b) for the second grade (Silver) = 50 combat days
c) for the third grade (Gold) = 100 combat days

5.   *Crediting of combat days:*
a) <u>For the members of all units committed in the infantry role:</u>
All days in which the members of the units have the opportunity to engage the enemy in close combat (man against man). This can involve attack, defense, patrols, service as a runner, combating enemy patrols, etc.
b) <u>For the members of heavy weapon units:</u>
All days in which members of these units (gun crews etc.) engage in direct action (close combat) with bandits.
For members of the flak arm engaged in the anti-bandit war, in addition to days in which gun crews etc. are engaged in direct action with bandits, also those in which the gun crews shoot down enemy aircraft.
c) For the crews of individual aircraft or aviation units engaged in the anti-partisan war:
All days in which the aircraft crews successfully carry out a mission under enemy fire. The confirmed shooting down of an enemy aircraft counts for 3 combat days.
The following number of combat days is required as condition for the awarding of the Anti-Partisan War Badge to aircraft crews:
for the first grade (Bronze) = 30 combat days
for the second grade (Silver) = 75 combat days
for the third grade (Gold) = 150 combat days.

Combat days could be calculated retroactively to 1 January 1943. Days that had already been awarded for the Close Combat Bar could not be used again for the Anti-Partisan War Badge. As fifteen close combat days had to be reached for the awarding of the 1st grade of the Close Combat Bar, only a maximum of 14 days could be retroactively listed.

On 4 August 1944 the Army High Command decreed that the Close Combat Bar could <u>only</u> be awarded for actions against regular enemy troops. Close combat against partisans was thus used <u>exclusively</u> to determine who received the Anti-Partisan War Badge. Until then, therefore, close combat against partisans could be recognized with the Close Combat Bar.

This was also the reason for the introduction of the new war badge. As it had obviously been decided that close combat against – for most part untrained – partisans/civilians could not be compared to actions against regular troops, more combat days were required per grade than for the equivalent grades of the Close Combat Bar:

Close Combat Bar		Anti-Partisan War Badge
1st Grade (Bronze)	15 close combat days	20 close combat days
2nd Grade (Silver)	30 close combat days	50 close combat days
3rd Grade (Gold)	50 close combat days	100 close combat days

Based on recommendations by company commanders, the commanders of independent battalions and regiments announced the credited combat days in the order of the day. Initially each man was supposed to maintain a supplementary page in his pay book, on which the company commander confirmed these action days. This was later abolished. In fact, misinterpretations of bandit combat days were common. Initially, days in which there was simple contact with partisans <u>without</u> close combat were counted. Several members of the *SS-Karstwehr-Battalion* who were awarded the Anti-Partisan War Badge stated that they had never experienced close combat with partisans. Former *SS-Unterscharführer* Wilfried Sonnenwald recalled:

> "Sixty-eight bandit combat days were confirmed in the supplementary page in my pay book by 16 June 1944. Some of these were probably struck off, for on 1 September 1944 I was "only" awarded the Anti-Partisan War Badge in Bronze for twenty bandit combat days. I must also say, however, that I never had a single close combat day with partisans. For us, every day in which we had enemy contact was counted as a bandit combat day."

When, on 25 August 1944, Himmler requested a report on those men who were supposed to receive the Anti-Partisan War Badge in Gold, this misinterpretation became quite obvious. The following message was then sent to the units that had submitted the recommendations:

> "The Reichsführer-SS has once again strongly emphasized that the strictest standards must be applied in ascertaining bandit combat days, and that only actual close combat days be used for awarding the Anti-Partisan War Badge."

On 9 March 1945 it was stressed once again that close combat days had to be used. This is documented by a letter written by *SS-Sturmbannführer* Wenner, the Senior SS and Police Commander in Italy:

> "With respect to this, I would like to once again stress that, in many cases, the information on which the recommendations are being based is derived from entries in pay books. Practice has shown, however, that the intent of

the regulations is being ignored when entering bandit combat days. Not only are close combat days being claimed as partisan combat days, but also days with the slightest enemy contact, even including nothing more than active duty days."

Former *SS-Sturmmann* Erwin Röslen recollects typical actions against partisans that were viewed by the men as partisan combat days. As they did not explicitly involve *"man against man"* action, despite their difficulty, they should not have been included in calculations for the Anti-Partisan War Badge:

"After we were placed on alert for an operation in the Görz-Ternova forest area, one evening in February 1945 we set off on foot. The most important things were in our combat packs. Everything else we left in our rucksacks in Tolmezzo, but we never saw them again. At first we had no idea where we were going or what our mission was. I still remember that it was a bitterly cold night. The next day we saw the last German fighter aircraft climbing away from a nearby air base. I mention this, because in the actions that followed, the Italian partisans were often supported by British aircraft. The latter dropped weapons, ammunition and food or attacked certain targets. Once, as we were climbing a mountain, we saw an attack by about six British aircraft armed with rockets on a town in which a police unit equipped with captured T-34 tanks was stationed.

It turned out that our mission was to relieve a police unit that was surrounded by partisans in a mountain town. We were met by heavy machinegun and rifle fire, but we were able to pin down the enemy with accurate heavy machinegun fire and after an hour freed the men of the police unit. One could clearly see the stress that they had been under in the past days.

Almost every day we watched enemy aircraft dropping supply containers. Those of us still with Italian weapons exchanged them for English weapons and ammunition. Their sub-machineguns were particularly sought after. All in all, because of the support they received, the partisans were better armed than we were. The area of operations, with its large, almost primeval forests, was especially treacherous and put high demands on us all.

One day, from our strongpoint we observed six aircraft dropping supply containers on the hills facing us. Prior to the drop we saw people, probably the inhabitants of the nearby town, laying out a cross that was probably supposed to mark the drop point. Even the priest in his black cassock was there. We decided to send an eight-man patrol to the drop site. We slipped through the intervening valley singly, at intervals of 250 meters, and then assembled on the enemy slope. Observations revealed that we were in the midst of the partisans. We advanced unseen to about thirty meters from the sentries. What we saw in the village and surrounding area made our hair stand on end. We identified about 400 partisans. So much for our dreams of a rich haul of booty. We decided that each pair of men would take different paths, so that if we were discovered one or the other might be lucky and make it through. Widely spaced, we headed back through the valley. On the opposite slope we stopped briefly to rest in a farmhouse. Suddenly a partisan appeared. A Croat who was part of our patrol wanted to capture him; but there was a brief exchange of fire and he was hit. We found him with a bullet in his liver. We fetched a ladder and a mattress from the house and tied our comrade to it. We also took the farmer with us so that he could show us the shortest way. Joining forces, we made it to a clearing. Just before this our "guide" jumped down a steep bank.

Because we were totally exhausted, we decided to rest a while before crossing the clearing. At a distance of ten to fifteen meters, we lay down and observed the clearing. The wounded man moaned from pain. Suddenly we heard a noise, and, in the light of the full moon, we saw twenty partisans at the edge of the wood, approaching in single file. We were unable to silence our comrade's groans. The partisans spotted us, raised their sub-machineguns and opened fire from pointblank range. The bullets passed over us – too high, thank God. None of us was hit. Our squad leader opened up with his sub-machinegun, and we also fired back with the light machinegun and carbines.

Suddenly, the partisans were gone as quickly as they had appeared. We waited for some time. When we could no longer see or hear anything, we prepared to cross the wide clearing. Then houses appeared before us, and we had to find out if the enemy was inside before we could go on. With hand grenades at the ready and covered by the squad leader with his sub-machinegun, we kicked the doors open. No partisans. We carried on, and after about an hour we came to a Wehrmacht security strongpoint with a twin-barreled anti-aircraft gun located on a road through the pass. From there the wounded man was driven back to our army comrades' position. He was beyond help, however. Completely exhausted, we lay down on the ground. After several hours' sleep we returned to our strongpoint. We had no booty, but we did return with information about the roads and the strength of the partisans."

In accordance with the different units, a variety of command positions were entitled to award the decoration, however Himmler reserved to himself the right to award the 3rd Grade – not least because of the reasons outlined:

a)   The *Reichsführer-SS*
b)   The Commander of Anti-Bandit Units for members of the staff of the Senior SS and Police Commander and all units of the police, *Waffen-SS* and *Wehrmacht* directly attached to him.
c)   The Senior SS and Police Commander for the units of the police, *Waffen-SS* and *Wehrmacht* directly attached to him.

d)   <u>The tactical superior with the authority of at least a division commander</u> for the army soldiers directly attached to him.

e)   <u>The Commander-in-Chief of a naval group or high command</u> for members of the navy.

f)   <u>The commanding general</u> for members of the *Luftwaffe*.

The badge could be awarded if the required conditions were almost met, provided the recipient was unable to reach the required number of bandit combat days because of wounds. In this situation approval was also reserved to the *Reichsführer-SS*.

The decoration could be awarded to any German soldier or foreign volunteer who had taken the oath to Adolf Hitler. As of 5 October 1944 the circle of personnel was expanded to those *"who are not members of the Wehrmacht, the Waffen-SS or police, but who have actively participated in actions against the bandits."* In addition to members of the state railway, forestry workers, who were often attacked by partisans in the many forests in occupied territories, could also theoretically be awarded the decoration.

As previously mentioned, it became apparent that most of the conditions for receipt of the decoration had been misconstrued. The following was written by the adjutant of the *Reichsführer-SS*, *SS-Sturmbannführer* Kment, to the Senior SS and Police Commander in Italy, *SS-Obergruppenführer* and *General der Waffen-SS* Wolff:

> *"In order for your applications for the awarding and presentation of the Anti-Partisan War Badge in Gold to be submitted to the Reichsführer-SS, the applications must first be carefully checked by the local command. The applications submitted by you on 27 September 1944, which are returned enclosed, do not create the impression that those recommended experienced man-against-man combat 100 times in the listed time periods."*

As this scrutiny did not occur until a submission was received for the awarding of the Anti-Partisan War Badge in Gold, it is safe to say that a considerable percentage of the Anti-Partisan War Badges in Bronze and Silver were awarded contrary to the statutes. In addition to the statements by former *SS-Karstjäger*, this is borne out by the awarding of the decoration to various senior officers and commanders. It may be assumed that the sixty-five-year-old commander of the *SS-Karstwehr-Bataillon*, *SS-Standartenführer Dr. Brand*, did not take part in 20 or 50 days of close combat against partisans. In addition to his extreme corpulence and a larynx condition, he had just one eye and it had pupillary rigidity. The awarding of the Anti-Partisan War Badge in Bronze must therefore have been in recognition of his previous service or because of misinterpretation of the term "bandit combat day" as previously mentioned. *SS-Gruppenführer* Globocnik, the Senior SS and Police Commander in the Adriatic Coastland Zone of Operations,[1] touched on this in a letter to Dr. Brand dated 23 February 1945:

---

[1] As the shorter wording "Senior SS and Police Commander Adriatic Coastland" was frequently used at the time, hereafter the text will also forego the "Operations Zone."

"Regarding your Anti-Partisan War Badge, I am pleased to inform you that it is already on its way to you and I hope that you have received it before this letter. Please accept my congratulations for the decoration. As the Waffen-Gebirgs-Karstjger-Brigade is no longer attached to me in any way, as per new orders, I had little influence in the awarding of the Anti-Partisan War Badge to you.

I must adhere to very strict guidelines from the Reichsführer-SS in procuring data for the awarding of the Anti-Partisan War Badge. I am sorry that the KJB [Karstjger-Brigade] was unable to provide any additional supporting data. I am therefore unable to effect any change, but I hope that you will be pleased with the Bronze ..."

A total of four members of the *24. Waffen-Gebirgs[Karstjäger]-Division der SS* were awarded the Anti-Partisan War Badge in Gold on 15 February 1945 and six on 9 March 1945. It can be assumed that none of these ten soldiers experienced 100 close combat days. With respect to *SS-Obersturmführer* Prasch, for example, the award application reveals that the information concerning close combat days was based on *"his own information."*

As the different number of combat days required for the three grades of the Anti-Partisan War Badge compared to those for the Close Combat Bar shows, so-called *"Bandenkampf"* (bandit fighting) was invariably less highly regarded than action against regular troops. There was also no *"automatic"* awarding of the Iron Cross, First Class or German Cross in Gold to wearers of the Anti-Partisan War Badge in Silver or Gold. While Hitler decreed that holders of the Close Combat Bar in Gold could automatically receive the German Cross in Gold with no further documentation, because fifty close combat days was sufficient evidence of conspicuous bravery and aggressiveness, prior to receiving the Anti-Partisan War Badge in Gold, seven of the ten recipients had not even received the Iron Cross, Second Class or the Wound Badge in Black (sic!). This was surely also proof that the 100 bandit combat days had not been close combat days.

Worn on the left chest, the badge's dimensions were 48x58mm. It had an oak leave wreath, in the center of which a Germanic sword stabbed a five-headed hydra. In Greek mythology the hydra was a nine-headed snakelike creature, which grew two new heads for each one that was cut off. Beneath the handle of the sword was a sun wheel and below the hydra a death's head.

Altogether there were seven manufacturing variants of the Anti-Partisan War Badge:

1. A heavy (full) version with a wide, bulbous pin. Its outstanding feature was three perforations in the area of the hydra.
2. A heavy (full) version with a wide, bulbous pin. This version lacked any perforations in the area of the hydra.
3. A light version with a wide, bulbous pin. There were examples of this version with two and three perforations in the area of the hydra.

4. A light version with a blunt, thin, round pin. There were two perforations in the area of the hydra.
5. A light version with a pointed, thin, round pin. This decoration was manufactured with three perforations in the area of the hydra.
6. A heavy (full) version of the Grade III of non-ferrous metal with the blade of the German sword bronzed as a special feature. This badge was made for presentation by Himmler.
7. A heavy (full) version of the Grade III made of silver with twenty-six small diamonds on the sun wheel. These twenty Anti-Partisan War Badges were probably intended for honorary awards, like the Combined Pilot's and Observer's Badges with Diamonds, for example.

With the exception of the last two versions, as a rule the Anti-Partisan War Badge was made of refined zinc and alloyed as per the grade.

The number of decorations awarded can only be estimated. As there were almost no partisan combat zones left apart from southeastern Europe and the *Generalgouvernement* (Poland) within about a year after the institution of the decoration, the potential number of recipients was small. Of the more than 500,000 soldiers and policemen engaged in protecting the rear area, probably about 3,000 in total received the badge in bronze, about 800 in silver and ten in gold.[2]

By comparison: of the more than 10,000,000 members of the army, only about 650 received the Close Combat Bar in Gold. The total number of close combat days required to win the decoration was fifty, exactly the same number needed for the Anti-Partisan War Badge in Silver.

---

[2] Also interesting in this respect is SS-Sonderkommando Dirlewanger, which was in constant action against partisans from the spring of 1942 until autumn 1944. After the Anti-Partisan War Badge was instituted, in February 1944 this unit requested twenty badges in gold, thirty in silver and 200 in bronze. In fact, by war's end none of its personnel were awarded the third grade of the decoration, while the Anti-Partisan War Badge in Bronze and Silver were only awarded in a handful of cases.

Light version of the Anti-Partisan War Badge in Bronze with a thin, blunt pin and two perforations in the area of the hydra.

BESITZZEUGNIS

DEM

SS-Sturmmann

Heinrich S c h n e i d e r

6./Waffen-Geb. (Karst) Jäger-Rgt.
SS-Nr. 59

VERLEIHE ICH
FÜR TAPFERE TEILNAHME
AN 20 KAMPFTAGEN

DAS

BANDENKAMPFABZEICHEN
IN B r o n z e

O.U.,DEN 30. Januar 1945.

SS - Gruppenführer
u. Generalleutnant d. Polizei

Hans Tonsor as an SS-Unterscharführer before the end of the war.

BESITZZEUGNIS

DEM

SS-Rottenführer

Hans T o n s o r

I./Waffen-Geb. (Karst) Jäger-Rgt.
SS-Nr. 59

VERLEIHE ICH
FÜR TAPFERE TEILNAHME
AN 20 KAMPFTAGEN

DAS
BANDENKAMPFABZEICHEN
IN B r o n z e

O.U.,DEN 30. Januar 1945

'A - Gruppenführer
u. Generalleutnant d. Polizei

Tonsor was a member of the signals
platoon of Headquarters, I Battalion,
59th Regiment. The award certificate
states that Tonsor was awarded the
Anti-Partisan War Badge in Bronze for
twenty bandit combat days.

Pages from the pay book of Johann Pierron, who was born in 1924 and in October 1942 was called up by the 2nd Company, SS Infantry Replacement Battalion Germania. A few weeks later he was transferred to the SS-Karstwehr-Bataillon.

A. Zuletzt zuständige Wehrersatzdienststelle: St. Wolla

E. St. Rhein XII, Wiesbaden

B. Zum Feldheer abgesandt von:[1]

	Ersatztruppenteil	Kompanie	Nr. der Truppen-stammrolle
a	2./SS. Inf. Ers. Btl. "Germania"		22545
b			
c			

C.

	Feldtruppenteil[2]	Kompanie	Nr. der Kriegs-stammrolle
a	SS Karstwehrkompanie	Kr. 204
b	SS Karstwehr Btl.	Stabsk.	Kr. 123
c	Waffen-Geb. Gr. Rgt. der SS 24		123
	Stabsk. I. Staffel Kav. Korp. 15-19 SS	

D.

	Jetzt zuständiger Ersatztruppenteil[2]	Standort
	SS Karstw.Kp.	
	SS Karstwehr Ers. Kp.	Pottenstein
	SS Karstjäger Ers. Komp.	Windisch-Bleiberg

(Meldung dortselbst nach Rückkehr vom Feldheer oder Lazarett, zuständig für Ersatz an Bekleidung und Ausrüstung)

[1] Dem Ersatztruppenteil einzutragen, von dem der Soldbuchinhaber zum Feldheer abgesandt wird.
[2] Dem Feldtruppenteil einzutragen und bei Versetzungen von einem zum anderen Feldtruppenteil derart abzuändern, daß die alten Angaben nur durchstrichen werden, also leserlich bleiben.

Weiterer Raum für Eintragungen auf Seite 17.

4

Anschriften der nächsten lebenden Angehörigen

des Johann Pierron
(Vor- und Zuname)

1. Ehefrau: Vor- und Mädchenname
(ggf. Bernert, ledig) ....

Wohnort (Kreis) ....
Straße, Haus-Nr. ....

2. Eltern: des Vaters, Vor- und Zuname ..... Josef Pierron
Stand oder Gewerbe Bergmann
der Mutter, Vor- u. Mädchenname
Marie-Anne Massing
Wohnort (Kreis) Kriechingen (Kr. Saarlautern)
Straße, Haus-Nr. Hartberstr. 2

3. Verwandte oder Braut:[*]
Vor- und Zuname ....
Stand oder Gewerbe ....
Wohnort (Kreis) ....
Straße, Haus-Nr. ....

[*] Ausfüllung nur, wenn weder 1. noch 2. ausgefüllt sind.

5

Pierron served in the Pioneer Company as well as in the Headquarters Companies of the I and II Battalions. He was awarded the Anti-Partisan War Badge in Bronze on 30 January 1945.

Auszeichnungen

Datum	Art der Auszeichnung	Verleihungsurkunde	Bestätigung des Komp.- usw. Führers, Dienstgrad
30.1.45	"Bandenkampfabzeichen" "Bronze"		SS Untersturmführer u. K. Führer

22

Beurlaubungen über fünf Tage
(Vor Urlaubsantritt auszufüllen)

1. Vom bis	Grad	
	den	
		(Unterschrift des Komp., Truppenführers usw.)
2. Vom bis	nach	
	Grund:	
	den	
		(Unterschrift des Komp., Truppenführers usw.)
3. Vom bis	nach	
	Grund:	
	den	
Dienststempel		(Unterschrift des Komp., Truppenführers usw.)
4. Vom bis	nach	
	Grund:	
	den	
Dienststempel		(Unterschrift des Komp., Truppenführers usw.)

HAT URLAUBERPAKET

23

Johann Pierron as an SS-Rottenführer wearing the Anti-Partisan War Badge in bronze.

BESITZZEUGNIS

DEM

SS-Sturmmann

Johann Pierron

I./Waffen-Geb-Karst-Jäger-Rgt.d.SS-Nr.59
Stabskompanie

VERLEIHE ICH
FÜR TAPFERE TEILNAHME
AN 20 KAMPFTAGEN

DAS

BANDENKAMPFABZEICHEN

IN Bronze

O.U., DEN 30. Januar 1945.

...ppenführer
...d. Polizei

Light version of the Anti-Partisan War Badge in Bronze with a broad, bulbous pin and two perforations in the area of the hydra.

Wilfried Sonnenwald

BESITZZEUGNIS

DEM

SS-Sturmmann

Wilfried Sonnenwald

Stabskompanie/SS-KWB.

VERLEIHE ICH
FÜR TAPFERE TEILNAHME
AN 20 KAMPFTAGEN

DAS

BANDENKAMPFABZEICHEN

IN Bronze

O.U. , DEN 1. September 1944.

Der Höhere ⚡⚡-u. Polizeiführer
in der Operationszone
„Adriatisches Küstenland"

⚡⚡ - Gruppenführer
Generalleutnant d. Polizei

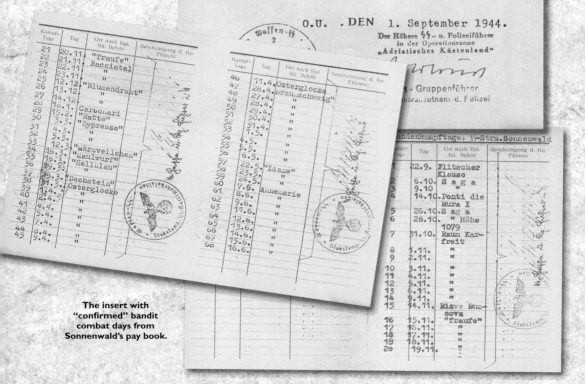

The insert with "confirmed" bandit combat days from Sonnenwald's pay book.

Erwin Röslen (standing) with an 81.4mm mortar.

BESITZZEUGNIS

DEM

SS- Sturmmann

Erwin Röslen

8./Waffen-Geb. (Karst) Jäger-Rgt.

SS-Nr. 59

**VERLEIHE ICH
FÜR TAPFERE TEILNAHME
AN 50 KAMPFTAGEN**

DAS

BANDENKAMPFABZEICHEN

IN Silber

O.U., DEN 30. Januar 1945.

ℋ - Gruppenführer
u. Generalleutnant d. Polizei

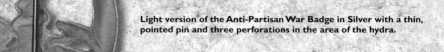

Light version of the Anti-Partisan War Badge in Silver with a thin, pointed pin and three perforations in the area of the hydra.

SITZZEUGNIS

DEM

SS-Unterscharführer

Alfred T i e f e n b a c h e r

6./Waffen-Geb. (Karst) Jäger-Rgt.

SS-Nr. 59

VERLEIHE ICH
FÜR TAPFERE TEILNAHME
AN 50 **KAMPFTAGEN**

DAS
BANDENKAMPFABZEICHEN
IN S i l b e r

O.U. ,DEN 15. Februar 1945.

SS - Gruppenführer
u. Generalleutnant d. Polizei

Heavy version of the Anti-Partisan War Badge in Silver with a
broad, bulbous pin and three perforations in the area of the hydra.

Conversation with a Slovenian domobrani (Home Guard).

BESITZZEUGNIS

DEM

SS-Oberscharführer

Franz Ludwig

5./Waffen-Geb. (Karst) Jäger-Rgt.
SS-Nr. 59

VERLEIHE ICH
FUR TAPFERE TEILNAHME
AN 50 KAMPFTAGEN

DAS

BANDENKAMPFABZEICHEN
IN Silber

O.U.,DEN 30. Januar 1945

ührer
. Polizei

Headquarters Company omnibus. Second from the left is the Stabsscharführer.

The Anti-Partisan War Badge in Gold

Although the combat days required to earn the Anti-Partisan War Badge could be calculated retroactive to 1 January 1943, it was almost impossible to reach the necessary figure of 100 close combat days. For one thing, the nature of partisan warfare made close combat rare, while the probability that a soldier would survive 100 days in close combat – to the finish – with pistol, bayonet or entrenching tool, was slight.

As previously stated, the Close Combat Bar in Gold was awarded to about 650 soldiers who amassed fifty confirmed close combat days. The number of those who reached 100 close combat days against regular enemy troops was almost zero, however, as in the case of the Anti-Partisan War Badge.

To date, only ten soldiers are known to have been awarded the Anti-Partisan War Badge in Gold. All came from the same unit, the *24. Waffen-Gebirgs[Karstjäger]-Division der SS*. The majority of their partisan combat days took place in the summer of 1944, when they were deployed in small partisan-hunting detachments in the Tolmezzo area.

On looking through the files, however, one gets the impression that, in the case of these men, the award requirements were also interpreted loosely. Most had won no decorations at all before receiving the Anti-Partisan War Badge, and in most cases an application for the Iron Cross, Second Class was first made as part of the report to the *Reichsführer-SS*. In the award applications one can find handwritten notes in the margins that indicate serious skepticism on the part of the senior command headquarters. For example, in the award submission for *SS-Unterscharführer* Josef Weber, who had also been put up for the Anti-Partisan War Badge, one can find the succinct entry next to the passage claiming that he had spent a year in action against partisans:

"No! This would mean that Weber was in close combat every third day!"

The fact that it was almost impossible to reach the required number of close combat days makes it simple to understand why the Anti-Partisan War Badge in Gold was one of the rarest decorations of the Third Reich.

The first decorations were awarded by Himmler on 15 February 1944. The Berlin edition of the *Völkische Beobachter* of 22 February 1945 reported:

"On behalf of the Führer, the Reichsführer-SS also for the first time presented the Anti-Partisan War Badge in Gold to four members of the SS stationed in the Adriatic Coastland, specifically to

SS-Obersturmführer Erich Kühbandner
SS-Obersturmführer Helmut Prasch
SS-Hauptscharführer Alfred Ludl and
SS-Sturmmann Rudi Brauer

Instituted by the Führer, the Anti-Partisan War Badge, which is awarded in the three grades Bronze, Silver and Gold for 20, 50 and 100 combat days, acknowledges the efforts of the men engaged in fighting bandits. This fighting is one of the most difficult types of combat in the war. It is waged by relatively small units which are entirely on their own while pacifying large and difficult-to-reach areas, carrying out their operations against a cruel and devious enemy out of direct contact with centers of supply."

On 9 March 1945, the Anti-Partisan War Badge in Gold was awarded to six more *SS-Karstjäger*. This time the decorations were presented by *Generaloberst* Guderian at the Army High Command's command center in Zossen. Decorated were:

SS-Sturmmann Richard Armstark
SS-Unterscharführer Friedrich Fabel
SS-Sturmmann Michael Götzinger
SS-Sturmmann Johann Motz
SS-Unterscharführer Kurt Sinemus
SS-Oberscharführer Oswald Walter

Why all ten recipients were *SS-Karstjäger* can probably be explained by Himmler's realization that his grotesque idea of awarding a decoration for 100 close combat days was not feasible. And so these men, members of "his" *Waffen-SS*, were elevated for propaganda purposes.

In the end, further awarding of the decoration was prevented by the surrender of the German armed forces on 9 May 1945.

Brief Biographies of the Recipients

Richard Armstark was born in Luck on 19 September 1924 and in 1942 joined the *SS-Karstwehr*. He had been decorated with the Wound Badge in Black, the Infantry Assault Badge in Silver and the Iron Cross, Second Class before receiving the Anti-Partisan War Badge in Gold on 9 March 1945.

Rudi Brauer was born in Frankfurt/Main on 28 October 1925 and in 1945 was a member of the *Waffen-Gebirgs[Karstjäger]-Brigade der SS*. Already a wearer of the Wound Badge in Black, the Infantry Assault Badge in Silver and the Anti-Partisan War Badge in Bronze, on 22 January 1945 he was recommended for the Iron Cross, Second Class:

"SS-Rottenführer Brauer, faithful and trustworthy, has demonstrated outstanding personal bravery on several occasions during a year in action against bandits. During an assault on an Italian barracks on 9 September 1943, SS-Rottenführer Brauer, then a heavy machinegunner, was positioned with his weapon in a flanking position. He placed his gun in an open firing position close to the objective. The first and third gunners were wounded and put out of action. Though himself wounded in the face, he fearlessly continued operating his heavy machinegun and played an important part in the successful taking of the barracks. While serving as company headquarters runner, more than once he fearlessly delivered reports through kilometers of bandit territory, and during encounters with the enemy never backed down from a firefight. An application has been sent to the Reichsführer-SS for the awarding of the Anti-Partisan War Badge in Gold to SS-Rottenführer Brauer. He is worthy in every respect to receive the Iron Cross, Second Class."

On 15 February 1945 – even before he was awarded the Iron Cross, Second Class on 3 April 1945 – Brauer received the Anti-Partisan War Badge in Gold.

Friedrich Fabel was born in Württemberg in 1924 and in 1942 he joined the *Waffen-SS*. He attained the rank of *SS-Unterscharführer* in the *24. Waffen-Gebirgs[Karstjäger]-Division der SS*. He was awarded the Anti-Partisan War Badge in Gold on 9 March 1945.

Michael Götzinger was born in Romania in 1925 and was a member of the German ethnic group. After the international agreement on recruiting ethnic Germans for service in the *Waffen-SS*, on 13 May 1943 he volunteered and in the summer of 1943 joined the *SS-Karstwehr-Bataillon* by way of *SS-Grenadier-Ersatz-Bataillon "Ost." SS-Sturmmann* Götzinger was awarded the Anti-Partisan War Badge in Gold on 9 March 1945.

Erich Kühbandner was born in Rosenheim on 21 October 1921. After graduation, on 15 September 1939 he joined the 4th Company of the *SS-Ersatz-Bataillon "Deutschland."* From 10 January 1940 he served with the 8th Company of the *SS-Regiment (mot.) "Deutschland"* and on 1 March 1940 he was sent to the SS non-commissioned officers school "Radolfzell." Two months later he was transferred to the *SS-Junkerschule* in Tölz. He was promoted to *SS-Standartenoberjunker* on 9 November 1941. On 30 January 1942 Kühbandner was promoted to *SS-Untersturm*führer in the 6th Company of the *SS-Regiment (mot.) "Deutschland."* Seriously wounded on the Eastern Front, in June 1942 Kühbandner returned to the *SS-Ersatz-Bataillon "Deutschland"* and on 5 September 1942 was transferred from there to the *SS-Karstwehr-Bataillon*. On 9 November 1943 he was promoted to *SS-Obersturmführer* and awarded the Iron Cross, Second Class. The Iron Cross, First Class followed on 8 March 1944. The following is from the award application:

"Kühbandner distinguished himself through exceptional initiative and exemplary bravado in the fiercely-contested Flitsch-Karfreiter bandit area. During the decisive battle from 26 to 30 October 1943, the heavy weapons under his command, including mountain and infantry guns, provided effective support to the other arms under heavy counter fire, making it possible for them to reach the attack objectives more quickly than anticipated. During the assault on Karfreit on 31 October 1943, during which K. was given command of the 2nd Company, his energy and fierce offensive spirit enabled him to be the first to enter the town, which was occupied by a large number of partisans and fiercely defended from every house, and take possession of it in conjunction with the 1st Company, which arrived later. The following night an approximately 800-strong group of partisans launched fierce counterattacks in an attempt to retake Karfreit. Leading an attack force from Idreska, K. boldly and decisively drove into the middle of the enemy concentrations, scattering them in all directions and inflicting significant casualties. This brave and decisive act enabled Karfreit to be held and operations continued by follow-up troops. Having already been seriously wounded in the east and having forced the surrender of the Ugowitz barracks near Tarvis singlehanded, for which he received the Iron Cross, Second Class, in view of his exemplary personal actions in the described actions and the most recent combat operations at Emta, Bischofslack and Attimis, he is deserving of a very special decoration for bravery."

From 15 August to 16 November 1944 he led the *SS-Karstwehr-Ersatz-Kompanie* and was then transferred to *Waffen-Gebirgs[Karstjäger]-Regiment der SS 1* to command its newly-formed III Battalion. The III Battalion was disbanded on 7 February 1945 and Kühbandner was officially transferred to the *7. SS-Freiwilligen-Gebirgs-Division "Prinz Eugen."* In fact, he never served there and remained with the *24. Waffen-Gebirgs[Karstjäger]-Division der SS*. In the summer of 1944 Kühbandner was awarded the Anti-Partisan War Badge in Bronze (15 close combat days) and on 15 February 1945 was decorated with the Anti-Partisan War Badge in Gold. Officially he had taken part in 115 close combat days and survived!

Alfred Ludl was born in Sigmundsherberg on 26 June 1918 and on 1 November 1938 he joined the *SS-Standarte "Der Führer"* in Vienna. With the regiment, he took part in the campaigns in Holland, Belgium and France and on 8 June 1940 he was wounded while serving as a squad leader. On 1 April 1941 Ludl was promoted to *SS-Unterscharführer* and he subsequently saw action in the Balkans. In the Soviet Union he was wounded a second time and later joined the Convalescent Company in Stettin. From there, on 11 August 1942 he was transferred to the *SS-Karstwehr-Kompanie* in Dachau. There, on 1 June 1943, Ludl was promoted to *SS-Oberscharführer* and placed in command of a platoon in the 2nd Company, *SS-Karstwehr-Bataillon*. The following is from the award recommendation for the Iron Cross, Second Class:

> *"Platoon leader Ludl commanded his platoon in an exemplary fashion in the battalion's actions during the disarmament operation in the Flitsch-Karfreiter bandit area on 9 September 1943 and in the area between Baccia and the Idria Valley. His bravery and aggressiveness at Montemaggiore, which was also assessed as a close combat day by the le Fort security group and where he commanded the lead platoon, contributed to the success of the operation. Acting on his own initiative and quickly analyzing the situation, he took out an enemy heavy machinegun with his machine pistol, and he and his platoon made it possible for other elements to storm the village. Near Montemaggiore the company was able to engage a unit of more than 100 bandits, which was almost completely wiped out. More than 100 dead bandits were counted. Ludl also distinguished himself in other actions through his bravery and willingness and thus is fully deserving of this decoration."*

Ludl was awarded the Iron Cross, Second Class on 20 May 1944. Promoted to the rank of *SS-Hauptscharführer* on 1 April 1944, on 1 February 1945 he was put up for the Iron Cross, First Class. The following is from the award application:

> *"Platoon leader and company commander Ludl has proved himself as a leader and comrade in every situation and in all types of terrain. Ludl is a daredevil and an inspiration to the men under his command. His aggressiveness and panache inspire his men, and it is rare for a bandit to escape an action in which he is involved. Ludl has already earned the Iron Cross, Second Class, Infantry Assault Badge in Silver, the Wound Badge in Silver and the Anti-Partisan War Badge in Silver. He has been recommended for the Anti-Partisan War Badge in Gold."*

Ludl was awarded the Iron Cross, First Class on 23 April 1945. This followed the awarding of the Anti-Partisan War Badge in Gold, which took place on 15 February 1945.

Johann Motz was born in Hungary on 26 December 1916. As a member of the German ethnic group, following the agreement between Germany and Hungary signed on 1 February 1942 he volunteered for service in the *Waffen-SS*. He served in the *SS-Karstwehr-Bataillon* and on 15 February 1945 was awarded the Anti-Partisan War Badge in Gold. His ultimate rank was *SS-Rottenführer*.

Helmut Prasch was born in Weissenbach on 16 September 1910. After completing high school he worked as a teacher and district school inspector. From 27 December 1939 to 25 January 1941 he served in the *Waffen-SS* as an *SS-Rottenführer d.R.* and then moved to the Reich Main Security Office. There he was promoted to *SS-Untersturmführer* on 1 September 1941. Prasch then served the security police and security service in the Stein post (Slovenia). As commander of a self-defense battalion of the *Wehrmannschafts-Standarte Stein*, he took part in numerous actions against Slovenian resistance groups. On 22 and 23 May 1942 he was wounded twice in the extensive wooded area around Jantsch Mountain (Janče, approx. ten km west of Litija/Littai) and was awarded the Wound Badge in Black. On 2 March 1943 he rejoined the *Waffen-SS* and on 20 April 1943 was promoted to *SS-Obersturmführer*. After Italy's surrender on 8 September 1943 and the occupation of the country by the *Wehrmacht*, Prasch was transferred to from the Eastern Front to the province of Julish Venezia and named head of the security police and security service post in Pola. His office was under the Commander of the Security Police and SD in the Adriatic Coastland Zone of Operations based in Trieste. In late summer 1944 he was transferred to the *24. Waffen-Gebirgs[Karstjäger]-Division der SS* then being formed. When the institution of the Anti-Partisan War Badge was announced in the spring of 1944, he reported ninety-one previous bandit combat days! He claimed:

> *"In Russia as a patrol leader with the SS Panzer-Aufklärungs-Abteilung "Das Reich" under the command of SS-Obersturmführer Resch: 9 combat days*
> *In Upper Carniola with the commander of the Security Police and the Security Service post in Stein: 8 combat days*
> *In Upper Carniola as leader of the SS-Selbstschutz-Bataillon: 16 combat days*
> *In Upper Carniola as part of the Gendarmerie-Kompanie (mot.) "Alpenland" 2 under the command of Hauptmann Buchberger: 2 combat days*
> *In Upper Carniola as part of SS-Polizei-Regiment 18 under the command of Hauptmann Rehbein: combat days*
> *In Istria with the Waffen-SS as part of Sonderkommando SS Obersturmführer Mayr: 7 combat days*
> *In Istria as detachment leader: 45 combat days"*

In the course of his application for the Anti-Partisan War Badge in Gold, his record was also checked to determine if he was eligible for a higher grade of the Iron Cross. He was subsequently awarded the Iron Cross, First Class on 1 December 1944. After receiving the Anti-Partisan War Badge in Gold on 15 February 1945, the propaganda newspaper *Adria Illustrierte*, which was published in Trieste in several languages, reported:

> *"The first wearer of the Anti-Partisan War Badge in Gold in the coastland! After more than 100 actions, SS-Obersturmführer Prasch received the prestigious decoration from the Reichsführer-SS personally."*

Kurt Sinemus was born in Magdeburg on 7 August 1924 and saw action in the Soviet Union as a squad leader in the Reich Labor Service. Drafted into the *Waffen-*

SS, he went to Italy with the *SS-Karstwehr-Bataillon* on 9 September 1943. With the rank of *SS-Sturmmann* he led a squad in the 2nd Company. The following is from the award application for the Iron Cross, Second Class:

> *"With courage and bravery, Sinemus knows how to inspire his squad with his fighting spirit and spur it to a high level of performance.*
>
> *In the action at Rudani on 11 April 1944, Sinemus led his men with particular vigor and took two resistance nests in close combat, seriously weakening the bandits and facilitating the advance by the platoon.*
>
> *Sinemus has proved himself worthy of the Iron Cross, Second Class through the outstanding leadership of his squad and the offensive spirit he displays in every action, and I recommend that he receive the decoration."*

SS-Unterscharführer Sinemus was awarded the Anti-Partisan War Badge in Gold on 9 March 1945.

Oswald Walter was born in Friedland/Isargebirge on 12 September 1922. As a member of the *Waffen-SS*, he took part in the campaigns in Poland, Holland, Belgium and France. He was wounded on 27 May 1940. In 1942 he was transferred to the *SS-Karstwehr-Kompanie* and later to the 2nd Company, *SS-Karstwehr-Bataillon*. Holding the rank of *SS-Unterscharführer*, he acted as company headquarters squad leader. The following is from the award application for the Iron Cross, Second Class:

> *"Displaying a high level of professionalism and tireless bravado as company headquarters squad leader, he is always an example to his men.*
>
> *During the attack on Monte Ben on 14 June 1944, on the heights the lead group of 20 men engaged a far superior bandit force in a 1½-hour firefight in which Walter performed extremely well. Motivated by great bravado, he and a handful of men reached the hill and destroyed the enemy positions in close combat. On his own initiative, despite the enemy's superior numbers he and his small force pursued the fleeing bandit forces, achieving a great success without loss to the company and ensuring that the company attack could proceed quickly. SS-Unterscharführer Walter has proved himself worthy of the Iron Cross, Second Class and I recommend that he receive the decoration."*

Walter was decorated with the Anti-Partisan War Badge in Gold on 9 March 1945.

The following three members of the *24. Waffen-Gebirgs[Karstjäger]-Division der SS* were also recommended for the Anti-Partisan War Badge in Gold; however, as they ultimately failed to meet the requirements, they did not receive the decoration. They were, however, awarded the Iron Cross, Second Class on 3 April 1945. These were soldiers who were recommended for the 3rd Grade of the anti-partisan decoration even though some had not a single decoration – not even the Wound

BESITZZEUGNIS

DEM

ᚤ-Obersturmführer

Erich Kühbandner

III./Waffen-Geb.(Karst) Jg.Rgt.-ᚤ Nr.1

Adriatisches Küstenland

VERLEIHE ICH
FÜR TAPFERE TEILNAHME
AN 100 KAMPFTAGEN

DAS
BANDENKAMPFABZEICHEN

IN   Gold

reld-Kommandostelle, DEN 11. Februar 1945

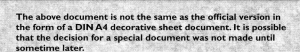

The above document is not the same as the official version in the form of a DIN A4 decorative sheet document. It is possible that the decision for a special document was not made until sometime later.

The heavy Anti-Partisan War Badge in Gold without perforation in the area of the hydra is a piece that SS-Obersturmführer Kühbandner purchased from a decorations maker after he was awarded the war badge.

SS-Obersturmführer Kühbandner

SS-Obersturm-
führer Prasch

This version of the Anti-Partisan War Badge in Gold with bronzed pin was awarded
to ten recipients on 15 February and 9 March 1945.

The Anti-Partisan War Badge in Gold with Diamonds.

Just twenty examples of the Anti-Partisan War Badge in Gold with Diamonds were made by the C.E. Juncker Company of Berlin. Made of silver, the badge had twenty-five small diamonds on the sun wheel and was probably intended for honorary presentations.

BESITZZEUGNIS

DEM

SS-Obersturmführer

Erich Kühbandner

2./SS-KWB.

VERLEIHE ICH
FÜR TAPFERE TEILNAHME
AN 50 KAMPFTAGEN

DAS

BANDENKAMPFABZEICHEN

IN Silber

O.U. .DEN 1. September 1944.

Der Höhere ⚡⚡- u. Polizeiführer
in der Operationszone
„Adriatisches Küstenland"

⚡⚡- Gruppenführer
u. Generalleutnant d. Polizei

Spring 1944: SS-Obersturmführer Kühbandner (hidden) with SS-Standartenführer Dr. Brand, riding through a village wrecked in fighting.

Badge in Black. It should be mentioned that the majority of the *SS-Karstjäger* decorated with the Anti-Partisan War Badge in Bronze and Silver also did not have the Wound Badge or Iron Cross.

Ewald Remmert was born in Falkendiek on 12 February 1924 and was a member of the *SS-Karstwehr* from the beginning. The following is from the award application for the Iron Cross, Second Class dated 22 January 1945:

> *"During a year of anti-bandit operations, SS-Unterscharführer Remmert has distinguished himself several times through fearless bravado and personal bravery while serving as squad leader. In the 1st Platoon's attack on Rudani (Istria), which was the base of the bandit leader of Pisino, it was Remmert who, alone with his squad, killed fourteen of the enemy and captured two light machineguns and 1,500 rounds of ammunition. During pursuit of the fleeing bandits, Remmert charged after them with his machine pistol singlehanded, and with his last rounds silenced a light machinegun nest that was still resisting stubbornly, capturing a sub-machinegun in the process. He resumed his pursuit and shot the fleeing bandit leader, a major.*
>
> *Remmert has the Anti-Partisan War Badge in bronze and I recommend that he be awarded the Anti-Partisan War Badge in Gold."*

Josef Weber was born in Etzlingen on 4 March 1923 and attained the rank of *SS-Unterscharführer* with the II Battalion, *Waffen-Gebirgs[Karstjäger]-Division der SS 59*. The award application for the Iron Cross, Second Class dated 22 January 1945 states:

> *"Faithful and trustworthy, in a year of anti-bandit operations SS-Unterscharführer Weber has distinguished himself several times through his conspicuous acts of personal bravery. A fearless daredevil, while serving as a runner in the company headquarters squad, he several times delivered messages through kilometers of bandit territory and in encounters with the enemy never backed down from a firefight. During an operation in the Tolmezzo area under SS-Obersturmführer Hesselbarth, while delivering a vital message to the battle group command post he ran into an enemy machinegun team. Weber overpowered the enemy, shot the four bandits and returned with the machinegun.*
>
> *Weber is recommended for the Anti-Partisan War Badge in Gold. Weber possesses the Infantry Assault Badge in Silver."*

Bernhard Wessels was born in Friesland on 10 April 1924 and on 26 February 1943 was mustered by the *Waffen-SS* replacement office in Hamburg. After being called up by the *Waffen-SS*, he served in the *SS-Karstwehr-Bataillon*. There he attained the rank of *SS-Unterscharführer* and on 3 April 1945 was awarded the Iron Cross, Second Class.

The History of the *24. Waffen-Gebirgs[Karstjäger]-Division der SS*

The Origins of the *SS-Karstwehr*

Interestingly, the roots of the later *24. Waffen-Gebirgs[Karstjäger]-Division der SS* are to be found in the civilian world. On 1 January 1935 the *Deutsches Ahnenerbe*, an ancestral heritage research association, was founded in Berlin. In addition to *Reichsführer-SS* Himmler, its creators included Dr. Herman Wirth, originally from the Netherlands. In the 1920s he had a built up collection dedicated to "*folkloristic customs and ancient beliefs*" and in 1932 established the Institute for Ancestral Heritage in Bad Doberan. Wirth had developed the theory that the Germans had lived peacefully in a matriarchal social order during the Neolithic period and sought a return to this "primitive state." Himmler, who presided over the research association, was very interested in Wirth's research, but he rejected the goal of a matriarchy. As the two could not agree, in 1938 Dr. Wirth lost his position with the research association, which on 1 January 1939 was renamed the *Das Ahnenerbe* Ancestral Heritage Research and Teaching Society (*Das Ahnenerbe*, literally "something inherited from the forefathers"). Its priority assignment was now to investigate the "*range, spirit, deeds and heritage of the Nordic Indo-Germanic people.*" In April 1940 the research and teaching society was incorporated into the personal staff of the *Reichsführer-SS*.

In July 1937 Himmler directed the research association to conduct a systematic inventory and investigation of caves in Germany. His goal was to provide archaeological evidence for historical research.

Two months after Austria was incorporated into the German Reich in March 1938, a Research Establishment for the Study of Karsts and Caves was established in Salzburg. In March 1939 this research facility was moved to Munich. The director of the institution, was concerned with:

- general investigation of karsts and caves,
- karst geology
- ancient and prehistoric speleology with special emphasis on anthropology, zoology and botany, and
- study of caves for defense purposes

Dr. Hans Brand was the cave researcher.

(Translator's note: Karst is defined as an area of irregular limestone in which erosion has produced fissures, sinkholes, underground streams, and caverns.)

In the course of military exploitation of civilian research facilities, in July 1942 the Institute for Military Scientific Applied Research was set up within the Ancestral Heritage Research and Teaching Society. Its tasks included

- chemical and biological warfare research
- military medicine research
- applied mathematics and plant genetics, and
- defense geology of importance to the war.

The new institute, the Research Establishment for the Study of Karsts and Caves, was repurposed for the latter field. Research objectives were modified to suit war requirements. The establishment's staff was now to determine to what extent caves could be used as armaments production sites safe from enemy bombs.

The *SS-Karstwehr-Kompanie*

When, on 1 March 1942, orders were issued for the formation of an SS volunteer mountain infantry division from ethnic Germans in the southeastern part of Serbia,[3] Dr. Brand, the head of the Research Establishment for the Study of Karsts and Caves in Munich, suggested to the *Reichsführer-SS* that his institution's knowledge be put to military use.

As the division's future area of operations against the widespread partisans was a karst region with all its geological peculiarities, Dr. Brand planned training courses in which the officers and non-commissioned officers would be taught all the military aspects of karsts and caves.

Himmler accepted the proposal and on 3 July 1942 ordered the formation of an *SS-Karstwehr-Kompanie* in the SS barracks in Dachau. Its strength was to be one officer, eight non-commissioned officers and sixty-five enlisted men. Dr. Brand, the sixty-five-year-old head of the Research Establishment for the Study of Karsts and Caves, was named company commander.

Initially the company was organized as follows:

- a karst training squad,
- a karst pioneer platoon and
- a karst Jäger platoon.

Preparations for the high mountain karst training courses began in the Toten Mountains near Alt-Aussee in September 1942 and ultimately barracks near Werfen-Wenig in the Tennen Mountains and in the Birgkarhaus on the Hochkönig were used. In addition to the high mountain karst courses, middle mountain karst courses were also supposed to be held in Pottenstein (Central Franconia), with the former hospital serving as quarters. Preparations for construction of a permanent training area finally began at the end of September.[4]

---

[3] SS-FHA, Org.Tgb.Nr.1268/42.

In October 1942 the members of *SS-Sonderkommando "K"* received mountain training. After the capture of the Caucasian oil fields near Maykop, Himmler had ordered the Ancestral Heritage Research and Teaching Society to investigate the Caucasus. A scientific expedition led by *SS-Sturmbannführer* Dr. Ernst Schäfer,[5] was supposed to conduct agricultural-botanical, zoological-entomological, geophysical and anthropological investigations of the entire Caucasus region. To this end, by order of the SS Command Central Office, *SS-Sonderkommando "K"* was formed in the SS barracks in Dachau effective 15 September 1942.[6] In addition to members of the *"Das Ahnenerbe"* Ancestral Heritage Research and Teaching Society, members of the *Waffen-SS* were attached to the unit as a security detail and received training in Pottenstein until mid-December 1942. Developments on the Eastern Front resulted in the cancellation of the expedition. With the end of the 6th Army at Stalingrad in sight, *SS-Sonderkommando "K"* was disbanded effective 29 January 1943.[7] The members of the *Waffen-SS* assigned to the *Kommando* ended their detached duty on 4 February 1943. The majority of them were assigned to the new *SS-Karstwehr-Bataillon*. Plans for the expedition were kept alive in the Ancestral Heritage Research and Teaching Society until January 1944 and were then also set aside.

Excursus: it cannot be assumed that the *SS-Karstwehr-Kompanie* was supposed to have taken part in "Operation Hercules," the invasion of Malta. In fact, however, rumors to this effect circulated among members of the unit. The later *SS-Sturmmann* Erwin Röslen remembered:

> *"Among others, we were supposed to take part in actions on islands in the Mediterranean. To this end we were supposed to learn to jump from an aircraft and land from the water. Developments in the military situation negated these plans."*

The action on Malta would have been theoretically possible, as the island has numerous karst features. The company's very specialized training would have been useful in such a situation. On 4 May 1942 Hitler gave the order for "Operation Hercules" to go ahead in July; at a time when the *SS-Karstwehr-Kompanie* had just received its formation order. Participation in the Malta operation would thus have been impossible. In any case, the 1,000 aircraft required for the airborne invasion would not have been available on account of the heavy fighting in North Africa. The occupation of Malta was postponed until a later date. Then in autumn 1942 the *SS-Karstwehr-Kompanie* was enlarged into a battalion and explicitly attached to the SS General Command (Tank). Any possible use in an action against Malta was thus excluded. In any event, the surrender of Army Group Africa that followed soon afterwards negated an occupation of the island.

---

[4] On 12 October 1942 inmates of the Flossenbürg concentration camp erected the Pottenstein I satellite camp. Those imprisoned there were then employed to build the barrack camp and a water training area. There were about 700 inmates in the satellite camp until 1945. Detachment leader SS-Oberscharführer Wodak was hanged on 22 September 1948 for his treatment of the inmates.

[5] Schäfer had led the German expedition to Tibet in 1938. Geheimnis Tibet, a film about the expedition, was shown in 1943.

[6] SS-FHA, Org.Tgb.Nr.5888/42.

[7] SS-FHA, Org.Tgb.Nr.154/43.

Dammaufschüttung
mit späterer Anpflanzung

Wasserübungsänlage

Für Friedensverhältnisse vorgesehenes Erholungsheim
der Waffen 44

44 Barackenlager

Burg Gößweinstein

Burg Pottenstein

Vorhandenes
Felsenschwimmbad

Weiherstal

Baracken - Gelände
der 44-Karstwehrtruppe

Anfahrt

1. Komp.

Gerüte - 9.

Waschhaus

Stabs - Komp

Stabs-9.

3.
Komp

Hochbehälter

Wasserbehälter

Wasserleitung
Pumpenhaus

2. Komp.

Führer B. u. Wirtschafts

4. Komp.

Waschhaus

Standpunkt
für die
Ansichtsskizze

3 KFZ-Hallen
für 100 Fahrzeuge

1. Stalle für 350 Pferde
und Trag. Tiere

Exerzier- u.
Sport - Platz

Straßenverlegung

Km. 582,5

G.   W.

This drawing by SS-Standartenführer Dr. Brand shows the existing and planned installations at the Karstwehr Training Base in Pottenstein.

The highland karst in
the Pottenstein area.

The SS-Karstwehr-Bataillon's barracks in Pottenstein. At the bottom, the multi-purpose hall.

The Karst Pioneer and Karst Jäger
Platoons during training in Pottenstein.

The *SS-Karstwehr-Bataillon*

Formation

After the *SS-Führungshauptamt* issued orders for the formation of an SS corps headquarters[8] at the Bergen – Fallingbostel training camp,[9] in July 1942 it ordered its transfer to the 15th Army in northern France and ultimately to the Avillon area in the south of France. There the attached units were reorganized and prepared for action in the Caucasus. When it was found that the region contained extensive karst features, on 19 November 1942 orders were issued for the existing *SS-Karstwehr* to be expanded to battalion size and attached to the newly created SS Corps Headquarters (Armored).

As the formation order explicitly contained the wording "for the SS Corps HQ (Armored)," it was obvious that the unit was no longer envisioned solely as a training body. Instead, attached to the corps headquarters, it would be actively deployed in the area of the front.

On 30 November 1942 the new battalion's strength was four officers, twenty-six non-commissioned officers and 172 enlisted men, distributed as follows:

Headquarters:	1 officer	4 NCOs	2 enlisted men
Core Battalion Dachau:[10]	1 officer	8 NCOs	68 enlisted men
High Mountain Karst Training Squad Birgkarhaus:	1 officer	3 NCOs	28 enlisted men
Middle Mountain Karst Training Squad Pottenstein:	1 officer	9 NCOs	49 enlisted men
Motor Vehicle Section Pegnitz:		1 NCO	11 enlisted men
Guards for the Inmates in Pottenstein:[11]		1 NCO	14 enlisted men

Not until February 1943 were enlisted men strengths increased, when the approximately 100 SS members of the disbanded *SS-Sonderkommando "K"* were integrated into the battalion. Approximately 200 members of the *SS-Gebirgsjäger-Ersatz-Bataillon "Nord"* from Trautenau followed in March 1943, after which the *SS-Karstwehr-Bataillon*'s organization was as follows on 30 April 1943:

Headquarters:	3 officers	6 NCOs	1 enlisted man
Headquarters Company:	1 officer	27 NCOs	161 enlisted men
1st Company:	2 officers	9 NCOs	205 enlisted men
4th Company:	1 officer	5 NCOs	195 enlisted men

---

[8] On 14 September 1942, this corps headquarters was renamed SS-Generalkommando (Pz) for the officers of the SS Panzer Grenadier Divisions "Leibstandarte Adolf Hitler" and "Das Reich." SS-FHA, Org.Tgb.Nr.5639/42.
[9] SS-FHA, Org.Tgb.Nr.3110/42.
[10] It subsequently formed the SS Karstwehr Replacement Company.
[11] These had been detached by the SS Anti-Tank Replacement Battalion.

The battalion thus had a total strength of seven officers, forty-seven non-commissioned officers and 562 enlisted men. In January 1943, in response to the Soviet winter offensive, the SS Corps Headquarters (Armored)[12] was hastily ordered into the Kharkov area. As the battalion was not yet operational, it did not accompany the corps headquarters, instead remaining in Pottenstein. Himmler subsequently made new arrangements and ordered that, once its formation was complete, the *SS-Karstwehr-Bataillon* be transferred, initially to the area of Slovenia around the 2,863-meter-high Triglav. In the Julian Alps, the battalion would be attached to *SS-Gruppenführer* Roesener, the Senior SS and Police Commander "Alpenland" for use against Slovenian partisans.

However, at first the formation process dragged on. Not until June 1943 was it possible to form the 2nd Company from members of the SS Panzer Grenadier School in Posen-Treskau and the 3rd Company from Romanian ethnic Germans who had been conscripted into the SS Grenadier Replacement Battalion "Ost."

On 1 July 1943, Corps Headquarters, *V. SS-Gebirgs-Korps* was formed for use in the Balkans and the *SS-Karstwehr-Bataillon* was attached to it as a corps unit, as had once been envisioned for the SS Corps Headquarters (Armored).[13] The battalion was to be employed against the numerous partisan formations operating in the Croatian and Serbian karst, along with the *SS-Freiwilligen-Gebirgs-Division "Prinz Eugen"* and the Croatian SS Volunteer Mountain Division. *SS-Standartenführer Dr. Brand*, the battalion commander, viewed this assignment skeptically. He wrote to Himmler, telling him that he thought that only a short-term deployment made sense, for *"if the intention is permanent inclusion within a mountain corps, then the further unhindered development of the SS-Karstjäger force and the associated expansion of the Karstjäger training facility in Pottenstein [...] would be placed in question."*

Subsequent developments saw to it that such wishes were not taken into consideration.

Into Combat 1943

The political upheaval in Italy, in which Mussolini was removed from his offices on 25 July 1943, triggered German countermeasures. They included reinforcement of the border crossings with Italy.[14] In the course of these reactions, the *SS-Karstwehr-Bataillon* was among the units placed on alert. It was subsequently transferred to the *II. SS Panzer Corps*[15] in the area around Villach, once again removing the unit from the new *V. SS-Gebirgs-Korps* then being formed. Attached to Battle Group Bredenförder of the 71st Infantry Division, the battalion was, however, under the

---

[12] As the result of the formation of another SS corps headquarters (armored), a Roman 2 was added to the designation, resulting in the title II SS Panzer Corps.

[13] SS-FHA, Org.Tgb.Nr.863/43.

[14] This included the alerting of so-called "Alaric units," troops that would disarm and intern Italian units in northern Italy after the codeword "Axis" was issued by the OKW.

[15] At the end of July 1943, Headquarters, II SS Panzer Corps was also moved from the Eastern Front to the German-Italian border area for Case Axis.

corps headquarters for which it had originally been planned in November 1942. The later *SS-Sturmmann* Erwin Röslen remembered:

> *"During July 1943 the necessary pack animals for us mountain infantry were brought from the horse collecting point in Kielce, Poland. They were Russian steppe horses and in pitiful condition. Thanks to good care, however, they later became faithful companions."*
>
> *Our training continued, and by mid-July 1943 it could be regarded as complete. Some of us were able to go on leave. Some were also employed to help the local farmers harvest their crops. One Sunday at the beginning of August, we were placed on alert status and made preparations to move out. Weapons and live ammunition were issued. A few days later we were put onto a train at Pegnitz station. No one knew where we were going, but we soon realized that we were headed south. Early the next morning the train stopped at the station in Arnoldstein near Villach, close to the Italian border. After getting off the train, the individual companies proceeded on foot to their assigned zone in the area of Gail Valley. The 4th Company was divided among the other three companies. We were quartered with the 1st Company in Feistritz. Our accommodations were in barns and tents. We had no idea why we had been moved and we were also not told.*
>
> *Combat training, often with live ammunition and mountain marches, was immediately back in the training program. After patrols to the border were planned, it slowly dawned on us. News filtered through that something wasn't right in Italy."*

After the Italian High Command sent additional troops to the border fortifications and prepared strategic sites for demolition, the reinforced 71st Infantry Division received orders to move into Italy on 26 August 1943. For the *SS-Karstwehr-Bataillon*, this meant crossing the border near Tarvis and a march into the Camporosso-Boscoverde area. There it was welcomed by the ethnic Germans living there and assumed responsibility for defending the Villach to Gemona section of the railroad.

The Italian High Command protested strongly against this independent action and declared that it would respond to any further unauthorized advance by German units into Italy with force of arms. The fracture of the former alliance was thus only a matter of time. On 30 August 1943, Army Group B was issued new orders for Case Axis, the withdrawal of Italy from the alliance. On receipt of the code word, the army group was to:

a) Reinforce all mountain crossing points
b) Occupy Genoa, La Spezia and Livorno, as well as Trieste, Fiume and Pola
c) Secure the most important Apennine crossings between Genoa and Florence
d) Pacify northern Italy.

On 7 September 1943, tensions between Germany and Italy reached such a point that Hitler decided to send the new Italian government an ultimatum. This contained a variety of demands that, if not met, would result in Germany taking additional steps for the security and conduct of military operations by its troops in Italy. The note was superfluous, for the next day the Italian government announced a ceasefire with the Allies. As a result, "Operation Axis" began at 20:00.

As a result of this, on the night of 8-9 September the *SS-Karstwehr-Bataillon* was used to disarm Italian forces near Pontebba, Uggowitza and Raibel. As the latter followed the orders of King Victor Emmanuel II and now regarded their former German allies as the enemy, there was heavy fighting in places. The later *SS-Sturmmann* Erwin Röslen remembered:

> *"Two or three weeks later, we were again alerted in the middle of the night. On foot with full packs, we moved with other troops towards the border and crossed in the direction of Tarvisio. We were on our feet almost all night and the following day. Just before nightfall we took up quarters in some houses and a meadow above Tarvisio. Our dreams of sleep were soon shattered. We were deployed by squads to defend important points. We noted that they were also being guarded by the Italians.*
>
> *During the night of 8-9 September we were quick-marched from our sentry positions back to our quarters. The company assembled there. We set off at a fast march with full pack in the direction of Tarvisio. In front of a telephone exchange (post office) we came under heavy rifle and sub-machinegun fire. In close combat, with support from a Wehrmacht light anti-aircraft gun, the resistance was quickly overcome. We carried on to a large army camp of the Italians, who had now become the enemy. After a few shots were fired, they surrendered without a fight.*
>
> *Soon afterwards we heard the sound of fighting to our rear. A runner arrived with orders for us to intervene immediately. We arrived to find that all hell had broken loose. The garrison of a large barracks, which also housed a general and his staff, was putting up a stiff fight. The building was on a slope and, with our light infantry weapons, could only be taken by direct assault. We met murderous return fire from close range. Without any cover, we fired our mortars from sixty meters, the shortest range possible. The fighting went on for hours and resulted in many killed and wounded.*
>
> *For us young soldiers – most were seventeen or eighteen years old – this was our baptism of fire, but we endured it with bravery. Our fallen comrades were buried in Camporosso near our battalion command post. It was difficult to say goodbye to comrades who had been forced to give up their lives in their youth."*

The later *SS-Rottenführer* Otto Walther described the events from his point of view:

> *"In July 1943 our battalion arrived in the area of Villach-St. Stefan in the Gail Valley-Nötsch-Feistritz-Arnoldstein. We were deployed in this area, which was near the Italian border. I was attached to the signals platoon, then made up of members of the 4th Company, and we were quartered in a barn in the middle of Arnoldstein. Day and night we were plagued by lice, fleas and other vermin. None of us knew what we were doing there. Then, in August, we crossed the border near Tarvis. We of the signals platoon went to Camporosso. The commander and his entire staff were in the Gasthof Post. Today this guesthouse has fallen into decay. We were in the center of town in a private house, under the roof. We were bitten and scratched in the straw, but there was nothing we could do about it. There was a barracks in Camporosso, just outside the town, occupied by Alpini, Italian mountain troops. There were also about 40 Carabinieri not far from our quarters. We had contact with the Italians, saluted, and when possible chatted. We were surprised, however, that they always had their weapons with them. Wherever they went, even into church, they took their weapons with them.*
>
> *At about 22:00 on the night of 8-9 September 1943, our platoon leader came and briefed us that there was going to be an attack against the Italians in the morning. It started at about four o'clock: we came under heavy fire. Several comrades and I were near the level crossing, which the national road still crosses today. Approximately fifty meters away was the Carabinieri barracks. We also saw officers and members of the staff and company.*
>
> *Then the Alpini opened fire on us from the barracks with mortars and heavy machineguns. The outburst lasted about thirty to forty minutes, then it was quiet. The Carabinieri and some of the Alpini came towards us with raised hands. They were rounded up and taken to the courtyard of the Gasthof Post to be shipped out. Unarmed officers and men stood among us and our headquarters staff. Our commander Dr. Brand had a lengthy conversation with a colonel of the Alpini. Our signals platoon was quartered in the small Alpini barracks. The nights that followed saw numerous skirmishes with the Alpini, who were still in the surrounding mountains and came down into the valley at night.*
>
> *Our losses in Camporosso amounted to sixteen killed. We secured some of the captured weapons, and when the battalion's motor pool was also moved up to Camporosso, we had considerable firepower.*
>
> *Several comrades and I were sent to guard our headquarters. We stood watch day and night. Except for a few incidents, not much happened there. Now and then in the morning, battalion commander Dr. Brand came out of the inn and brought us something alcoholic, to warm us up as he always said. He often put his arm around us and asked: son, did you have a good night? We called him Papa Brand and everyone liked him. The difference was still there however: the headquarters staff slept in beds and we lived*

in the barn next door in the straw with the lice, fleas and rats. The nights were not pleasant. A switchboard with about twenty lines was set up in the barn and manned constantly. During this time there was heavy fighting in the Karfreit-Flitscher Klause area in the area of the Isonzo. Our company deployed there took heavy casualties. Then our time in Camporosso came to an end. In November 1943 I rejoined my 4th Company, which was in Malborghetto, about 5 to 8 km west of Camporosso."

Using contemporary language, then *SS-Sturmmann* Emil Leininger wrote to his fiancé on 12 September 1943 and described the previous fighting:

"As you have heard on the radio, the Italians surrendered and were then called upon to lay down their arms. There was shooting in many places, but the macaroni soldiers came out on the short end. The SS never retreats."

On 16 September 1943, the commander of Battle Group Bredenförder (*Major* Bredenförder) composed a letter of appreciation for the attached *SS-Karstwehr-Bataillon*:

"Following the treachery of the Badoglio government, the German Wehrmacht, with its Battle Group Bredenförder, received orders to disarm the Italian army. In the sector held by the SS-Karstwehr-Bataillon, which since the march into Italy on 26 August 1943 has performed its task of guarding the important Villach to Gemona rail line in exemplary fashion, were located Italian garrisons that far outnumbered the battalion and which had at their disposal large stocks of weapons, ammunition, clothing and food. Nevertheless, early on 9 September 1943, after negotiations with the commander of the Italian troops failed to result in the majority of them laying down their weapons, the battalion attacked with outstanding zeal and took its assigned objectives, often in fierce close-quarters fighting. At 10:00 the battalion was able to report to the battle group that it had overcome the last resistance in Tarvisio. Sixteen brave SS non-commissioned officers and enlisted men had to pay with their lives for their willingness to fight. Fifty members of the SS-Karstwehr-Bataillon were wounded, some of them seriously.

This first action by the battalion demonstrated that its officers, non-commissioned officers and enlisted men are tough, determined fighters. I know that I can fully and completely depend on the SS-Karstwehr-Bataillon at all times."

During an inspection of the *SS-Karstwehr-Bataillon* in mid-September 1943, the commanding general of the *II. SS-Panzer-Corps* (*Obergruppenführer* Hausser) advised that the formation would be staying in the Tarvisio area for the time being. After the Italians had been disarmed, the unit secured the area against partisans. In the days that followed, the battalion repeatedly saw action in the Karfreit-Flitscher Klause area. The later *SS-Sturmmann* Erwin Rösler remembered:

"From that time on, the partisans, who had been joined by some of the Italian troops, became more active. In our area this happened at the Predil Pass and at the entrance to the Isonzo Valley. Generalfeldmarschall Rommel had fought there in the First World War. There, too, treacherous ambushes claimed victims. The high mountains (Triglav approx. 2,900 meters) and the difficult terrain made it easy for the partisans to escape. Tito's influence was already making itself felt in the partisan ranks. The red star and the words "Zivio Tito" (Long Live Tito) could be found everywhere. At that time we had no idea how treacherous the bandit war would become.

There was heavy fighting for the village of Saga and it was not until after about a week that it was taken, with support from the air force. Otherwise we only had our light weapons to fall back on. We subsequently cleared the enemy from the area as far as Tolmein."

The battalion's attachment to Battle Group Bredenförder of the 71st Infantry Division ended in the Pola area on 3 October 1943. It was then attached to Security Group le Fort (elements of the 188th Reserve Mountain Division). In recognition of its successful first action, in October 1943 Himmler awarded the Iron Cross, Second Class to members of the *SS-Karstwehr-Bataillon*. *SS-Sturmbannführer* Grothmann wrote of this from the *Reichsführer-SS'* field command post:

"From the list of recommendations for the Iron Cross, Second Class submitted on 24 September 1943, the Reichsführer-SS has approved the following:

1) *Bar to the Iron Cross, Second Class 1914 to SS-Standartenführer Dr. Brand*
2) *Iron Cross, Second Class to SS-Untersturmführer Weiland*
3) *Iron Cross, Second Class to SS-Hauptsturmführer Berschneider*
4) *Iron Cross, Second Class SS-Unterscharführer Meyer*
5) *Iron Cross, Second Class to SS-Oberschütze Tomasch*
6) *Iron Cross, Second Class to SS-Sturmmann Kuveke*

Enclosed are the decorations and award certificates with the request that you present them to those decorated."

The battalion's actions during this period are listed in the later award application for the Bar to the Iron Cross, First Class for *SS-Standartenführer* Dr. Brand:

"SS-Standartenführer Dr. Brand, commander of the SS-Karstwehr-Bataillon, served as part of the security group for anti-bandit warfare from 4 October to 15 November 1943. SS-Standartenführer Dr. Brand distinguished himself through conspicuous bravery and discretion in carrying out the tasks assigned to him. After the capture of Tarvis and the disarming of the Badoglio loyalist troops stationed there, the men of his battalion opened the Flitscher Klause and occupied Flitsch after overcoming stubborn resistance.

> *In the course of further operations, on his own initiative SS-Standartenführer Dr. Brand, with attached elements of the 139th Mountain Infantry Replacement and Training Battalion, cleared the Natisone Valley and the upper Isonzo Valley of bandits, making possible the restoration of the Rome - Vienna landline between Udine and Flitsch for the army group."*

The operations to liberate the two valleys of the Natisone and the Upper Isonzo were dubbed "*Wolkenbruch*" (cloudburst). During these operations the village of Strmc was burned down on 11 October 1943 in reprisal for partisan attacks in that area, and sixteen men between the ages of fifteen and fifty were shot. Still attached to the II SS Panzer Corps, the battalion next took part in "Operation *Traufe*," which began on 15 November. To deceive the enemy, the corps was designated the 1st SS Panzer Army (SS-Pz.A.O.K. 1). Together with elements of the 139th Mountain Infantry Replacement and Training Battalion, the battalion moved via Tolmein into the area west of Laibach. It was committed against powerful partisan units in the area around Logatec-Idria-Skolfia Loka-Val Baccia (Baccia Valley), with other units, including the 19th Police Regiment, taking part. After this operation ended on 20 November 1943, the unit saw action against escaped partisans in the area Sorica-Poce in the Baccia Valley. The later *SS-Sturmmann* Erwin Röslen remembered:

> *"At the beginning of November further areas, extending deep into former Yugoslavia, were cleared in conjunction with units of the Wehrmacht. As mountain troops, the task fell to us to go over the mountains, which were already covered in deep snow. Our pack animals could not go on, and we had to carry our equipment and ammunition ourselves. For weeks we faced extreme hardship. It was also very cold, especially at night. The action was ended at the end of November 1943 and our battalion was transferred to Gradisca."*

On 22 November the battalion received the order to join the *V. SS-Freiwilligen-Gebirgs-Korps*. *SS-Standartenführer* Dr. Brand opposed this vehemently, as he feared that his formation would lose its special status as a result. Thanks to another of his many letters to the *Reichsführer-SS*, he was able to gain approval for the *SS-Karstwehr-Bataillon* to remain in the area that had been assigned to it since the spring of 1943.

Four days later the unit was finally attached to *SS-Gruppenführer und Generalleutnant der Polizei* Globocnik, the Senior SS and Police Commander "Adriatic Coastland." On 1 December 1943, this was followed by the transfer to barracks in Gradisca d'Isonzo, (situated about sixty km to the southwest of Görz) and Sagrado. The later *SS-Rottenführer* Otto Walther remembered:

> *"At the beginning of December 1943 we were moved to, by our standards, large barracks in Gradisca. There our daily routine continued exactly as before, with drill, mock infantry attacks and parade marching. During*

that time some of our actions involved rail transport, but in most cases we travelled in our vehicles. Our trucks often transported us to the scene of the operation, with mules, weapons, ammunition and food. We then unloaded, often under fire from the partisans. In the mountains this sometimes took place in temperatures as low as minus 30-40 degrees Celsius."

As per Himmler's orders, in the new area the battalion was to:

• clear the area of partisans
• establish at least two permanent garrisons
• assist the Senior SS and Police Commander Adriatic Coastland in forming indigenous formations

In the second week of December, the 212-man-strong "Operations Company Kühbandner" was formed from elements of the Headquarters Company and the 2nd and 4th Companies. It took part in "Operation *Blumendraht*" (florist's wire) from the 12th to the 14th of December. As part of Battle Group von le Fort, the troops marched via Cergneu to Nongruella in the Nimes area (approx. fifteen km north of Udine), roughly forty-five kilometers distant. The operation involved numerous actions against partisans.

In December 1943 the members of the *SS-Karstwehr-Bataillon* saw firsthand the mercilessness of the partisan war. Then *SS-Sturmmann* Günter Stoschek remembered the day when 15 *SS-Karstjäger* were killed:

"On 26 December 1943 our platoon was alerted for a police action in the Görz area. In an area of positions dating from the First World War – just short of the area of operations – the platoon, which was riding in a truck, was ambushed by partisans. The place was called Biglia, if I remember correctly. Our platoon leader Conrad withdrew with the platoon in the direction of the area of positions, while Seitz and I covered the withdrawal with our light machineguns. As the road into the mountains behind the platoon had already been blocked by the time we withdrew, we fell back along the road we had driven in on. Some distance to the rear we came upon SS-Obersturmführer Kühbandner, who had been wounded in the foot, and two other comrades. Lichtmannecker was lying behind the company commander's vehicle. As we fell back, he called to us that a burst of machinegun fire had caught him in both knees. With him were three or four other comrades who showed no signs of wounds. As we had run out of ammunition for our machineguns and had no ammunition bearers with us, we were unable to provide any covering fire for our comrades. During the battalion action the next morning, we found two more comrades. Unwounded, they had been murdered and half buried. One of them was my second gunner, SS-Sturmmann Zerlach."

The later *SS-Sturmmann* Erwin Röslen recalled of this action:

"Christmas 1943, a platoon from our 2nd Company carried out a reconnaissance mission into the area beyond the town of Görz. This area was heavily frequented by partisans. The vehicles drove straight into a massive gathering of partisans and, if I remember correctly, only half of the approximately thirty men returned, some of them wounded. The rest were considered missing. A counteraction, in which I took part, was begun immediately but was unsuccessful. We found none of our comrades."

At the end of December 1943 the *SS-Karstwehr-Bataillon* in its base in Gradisca reported the following strength:

Officers	Non-Commissioned Officers	Enlisted Men	Total
8	117	821	946
0.08%	12.4%	86.8%	100%

The battalion was organized as follows:

Battalion Headquarters	approx. 20 men
Headquarters Company:	approx. 160 men
1st Jäger Company:	approx. 170 men
2nd Jäger Company:	approx. 170 men
3rd Jäger Company:	approx. 170 men
4th (Heavy) Company:	approx. 170 men
Artillery Battery:	approx. 80 men

The artillery battalion had been trained on captured Italian guns. While the battalion had an adequate number if enlisted men, it was short of officers and non-commissioned officers. Officers, in particular, were in particularly short supply, with approximately 60% of the authorized positions unfilled.

Operations in 1944

Because of the shortage of officers, only parts of the battalion took part in "Operation Edelweiss," which began on 15 January 1944. Once again the battalion was attached to Battle Group von le Fort. Initially with elements of the 188th Reserve Mountain Division, the SS men were first deployed in the area south of the Görz-Haidenschaft (Aidussina) line, which was thirty kilometers long. There was fighting in Lokve (approx. seven km NE of Tarnova), Predmeia (approx. fifteen km SE of Tarnova) and Chiapovano (approx. fifteen km NE of Tarnova). The operation against Slovenian partisans ended after fourteen days. After partisan quarters and depots were discovered in Lokve, the village of thirty-two houses was burned down and five inhabitants shot. "Operation *Enzian*" (gentian) followed almost immediately in the area around Monte Santo (NE of Görz), where there had been heavy fighting on the Isonzo Front during the First World War.

As at the end of November 1943, the *SS-Karstwehr-Bataillon* had been given the task of assisting the Senior SS and Police Commander Adriatic Coastland in the formation of indigenous units, on 6 January 1944 *SS-Obersturmführer* Dr. Brand suggested to Himmler that an *SS-Karstwehr* unit be formed from Slovenian volunteers:

> *"By training in Pottenstein, these people will get to know and value German character, and also gain contact with a German karst people engaged in a similar battle for survival. As a result, it will be easier to rid them of previous Bolshevik influences and ways of thinking. The extremely diligent, loyal, highly developable and close-to-the-soil Slovenian people, about whom I care very much, can then become an exemplary German protectorate under German control."*

The situation in the Adriatic Coastland was extremely unfavorable for recruiting, however. The communist partisans – which in 1941 had founded the Liberation Front (*Osvobodilna Fronta*) – controlled large parts of the country. While most of the population did not share their political views, after their previous experiences they were opposed to German-Italian policies. Attempts to rectify this situation resulted in the formation of the "Adria Detachment" within the *SS-Standarte "Kurt Eggers."* Small propaganda teams were supposed to win the natives over to the German side. The leader of *Einsatztrupp Görz, SS-Unterscharführer* Fuhrmann, described the situation as follows:

> *"In order for our propaganda to have a broader appeal, in various towns with Wehrmacht bases I have interested these units in our work and set up propaganda posts. Our materials are now delivered to them regularly. They accompany us during operations – patrols and the like – and thus deliver it to areas where, because of the bandit threat, we could never drive in our vehicles."*

Because of *SS-Standartenführer* Dr. Brand's pro-Slovenian attitude, the *SS-Karstwehr-Bataillon* also took part in the recruiting effort. Volunteers were taken in, as well as captured partisans who were forced to join. The former *SS-Sturmmann* Franz Holluschek remembered:

> *"Once, during an operation, we captured a young partisan: tall, blonde, blue eyes – we liked him. Initially we used him to carry four ammunition cans. Then four days later parts of the mortar and four weeks later one could see him strolling around in the barracks wearing an SS uniform.*
>
> *Brand also once formed a platoon of young Slovenians. Many came from families Brand had known in peacetime, when he researched the Slovenian karst. He said to them: give me your sons and nothing will happen to them.*
>
> *One day the Senior SS and Police Commander Globocnik saw them and wanted to take them with him to Trieste. Brand refused and told Globocnik*

that all thirty men would desert before marching off to Trieste. They were then divided among the individual companies so that they could no longer be found."

In addition, elements of the battalion were in action against partisans on an almost daily basis. In most cases this resulted from reports of partisans or clashes between German troops and partisans. The *SS-Karstjäger* were deployed in platoon strength to conduct reconnaissance or company strength to assist. On 15-16 February 1944, for example, the SS men took part in "Operation *Ratte*" (rat). Other units deployed south of Haidenschaft in the Reifenberg-Komen area included III Battalion, *SS-Polizei-Regiment 15* and units of the Commander of the Security Police. After members of the police unit were ambushed, the latter village was burned down and the population deported to the German Reich to work. The later *SS-Sturmmann* Erwin Röslen remembered:

> *"We had a terrible experience in February 1944. During the night we were alerted, in order to assist a police unit deployed in the karst region near Komen that had fallen into an ambush. But this we were unable to do. We found fifty-four men who had fought until their ammunition ran out. They had all been horribly mutilated. One of them, badly wounded, had previously managed to make his way to the nearest strongpoint. None of us who were there will ever be able to forget this picture."*

"Operation *Alpenrose*" followed from the 18th to the 21st of February 1944. Initially with elements of the *188. Reserve-Gebirgs-Division*, the *SS-Karstjäger* were deployed in the area between Tolmein and Cividale to engage two Slovenian partisan brigades with a combined strength of about 1,200 people. Elements of the *SS-Karstwehr-Bataillon* were temporarily encircled by the partisans during the heavy fighting. Sixteen members of the battalion were killed and thirteen wounded. Erwin Röslen remembered:

> *"Our 3rd Company walked into an ambush. We were able to free ourselves from the fatal encirclement, but only at the cost of considerable casualties and with appropriate support. Then the next day we found comrades who had defended themselves to the last round. They had been horribly mutilated. Several had perhaps taken own lives with their last rounds to escape the horror they would have faced as captives. The dead, those that we were able to find, were buried in the cemetery for German fallen of the First World War in Redipuglia near Trieste. After the war they were reinterred in Costermano.*
> *What we young soldiers saw and had to experience affected us deeply. We knew that there was no mercy for us if we fell into the hands of the partisans."*

From the 3rd to the 5th of March 1944, the battalion took part in "Operation *Zypresse*" in the Doberdo area (approx. six km SE of Gradisca). This was followed on 12 March 1944 by "Operation *Märzveilchen*" (sweet violet), which was followed by "Operation *Maulwurf*" (mole) four days later and "Operation *Hellblau*" (pale blue) on 18 March. All of these operations took place in the Komen area (approx. eighteen km east of Monfalcone).

On 23 March 1944 *SS-Hauptsturmführer* Berschneider took command of the battalion. After *SS-Standartenführer* Dr. Brand became convinced that he had the most experience in the karst and was thus best suited to wage war against the partisans there, he became involved in frequent disputes with the Senior SS and Police Commander Adriatic Coastland. Himmler subsequently relieved Dr. Brand of command of the battalion and placed him in charge of the new cave research facility in the karst. On 18 March 1944 Dr. Brand vented his feelings in one of his numerous letters to *SS-Sturmbannführer* Grothmann, Himmler's chief adjutant in his personal staff:

> *"After initial harmony with the Senior SS and Police Commander Adriatic Coastland, increasingly serious differences of opinion developed with respect to my necessary freedom of action and the tactically-correct employment of my unit.*
>
> *My forty-five years of military experience and my almost forty years of knowledge of the karst and its ethnic makeup mean almost nothing to him. Specialized knowledge of the karst is marginalized, contrary to the views of the Reichsführer-SS who sent me there for the tasks previously outlined. My SS karst force, whose specialized companies first became an operational unit when the battalion was formed, was torn apart and over the commander's head passed off to the Wehrmacht in small battle groups or even committed at discretion. If this worked, it was correct, if there was a failure, then it was blamed on the quality of the unit, for which its commander was held responsible. If the commander opposed such operational methods, which must result in the complete destruction of this valuable special unit, then he was viewed as troublesome or too old, and then the feuding began using every possible argument."*

The letter shows that Dr. Brand had misjudged the true situation. There was no place for such animosities in a war against superior materiel and numbers in which pragmatic decisions were required. The differences of opinion over fundamental command authority and responsibility for waging war against the partisans between Dr. Brand and Globocnik were not the only ones that existed at that time. There were also differences between Himmler and *Generalfeldmarschall* Kesselring, the Commander-in-Chief Southwest. For the sake of clarity, the *Wehrmacht* High Command declared that the entire effort against partisans in Italy was the responsibility of the Commander-in-Chief Southwest. But as *SS-Obergruppenführer Wolff*, the Senior SS and Police Commander in Italy who was subordinate to Kesselring, continued to act independently in the Alpine Foothills and Adriatic Coastland zones of operation, in practical terms command remained divided.

The *SS-Karstwehr-Bataillon* took part in "Operation *Dachstein*," which began on 25 March 1944, as the "Berschneider Group." Together with units of the 188th Reserve Mountain Division and the 15th and 19th SS Police Regiments, the men marched into Tarnova Forest (Zola-Adelsberg area). As was so often the case, however, no decisive success was achieved against the Slovenian partisans.

The large-scale, two-week "Operation *Osterglocke*" began on 31 March. It was the first action in Istria. The German command had come to fear an invasion of the peninsula by the western allies and wanted the rear permanently cleared of partisans. The Berschneider Group, together with police and *Wehrmacht* units, combed the Pisino area (Mitterburg in German, approx. forty-five km south of Trieste) to Albona (approx. thirty km SE of Pisino). The anti-partisan effort in Istria took on special importance as Tito wanted to bring the area under his influence from Croatia.

In addition to the companies of the *SS-Karstwehr-Bataillon*, others were deployed with *SS-Gebirgsjäger-Ausbildungs-und Ersatz Bataillon 7* to secure the area between Laibach and Trieste. For Hitler's birthday, the 20th of April 1944, the *SS-Karstwehr-Bataillon* was ordered to Trieste, where it took part in a parade before *SS-Gruppenführer und Generalleutnant der Polizei* Globocnik, the Senior SS and Police Commander Adriatic Coastland.

From 26th April to 6 May 1944 there was another operation in Istria that was dubbed *Braunschweig* (Brunswick). Together with elements of the 278th Infantry Division, the 181st Reserve Mountain Division and several companies from the 15th and Bozen Police Regiments, the *SS-Karstwehr-Bataillon* was committed in the area of Monte Maggiore[16] (Učka in Croatian) – Pivka Valley (Sankt Peter in German, approx. fifty km east of Trieste) – Brkini Mountains – Tschitschen Boden. About 1,800 (suspected) partisans were taken prisoner and 390 were considered "*destroyed*" in the fighting. German losses were minimal.

After this operation the *SS-Karstjäger* moved back to Gradisca, about ninety kilometers away. There, on 13 May 1944, the unit's former commander, *SS-Standartenführer* Dr. Brand, was given a farewell with military honors by *Gauleiter* Rainer and *SS-Gruppenführer* Globocnik. *SS-Hauptsturmführer* Berschneider, who had been leading the battalion in an acting capacity, became the new battalion commander.

From the 22nd to the 27th of May 1944, the *SS-Karstjäger* took part in "Operations *Liane I – III*" in the Peternel – Casteldorba (approx. twenty km north of Gradisca) area. This was followed by "Operation *Spitz*" near Reifenberg (approx. thirty-six km east of Gradisca) on 28 and 29 May. The latter was an action under the command of *SS-Obersturmführer* Kühbandner, who led a combined force made up of the 2nd and 4th Companies. Kühbandner had the pet name "Spitz" as he had a dog of that breed.

The large-scale "Operation *Annemarie*" began on 5 June 1944. From Baccia Valley (Batsch in German, approx. 22 km SE of St. Peter), the *SS-Karstwehr-Bataillon* marched through Görz, where for a time it guarded an Italian gas grenade

---

[16] This, the largest mountain on the peninsula, is approximately thirty km southwest of Fiume.

depot, and Haidenschaft into the Trieste area. Elements of *SS-Polizei-Regiment 10* also took part in the operation, in which thirty-nine partisans were captured and 108 killed in combat. German losses were three killed and twenty-three wounded. One Italian 105mm artillery piece with sixty rounds of ammunition, one light machinegun and one sub-machinegun were captured, giving rise to the question whether the 108 persons killed in combat had in fact been partisans. During the operation, on 11 June several captured partisans were handed over to the battalion by *Reserve-Gebirgsjäger-Regiment 139* and two of these were beheaded in Indrijske Krnice (approx. fourteen km east of Chiapovano). It therefore appears that the commander of *Reserve-Gebirgsjäger-Regiment 139* did not want to be burdened with their punishment. The later *SS-Oberscharführer* Franz Ludwig remembers:

> *"In June 1944 the Wehrmacht mountain infantry handed five partisans over to us for interrogation by the SD members attached to the SS-Karstwehr-Bataillon (1 officer, 1 NCO and 1 driver). During the interrogation, two were accused by the others of having repeatedly mistreated German prisoners in the past and of having murdered them in a gruesome manner. The accusations were made in such detail that the two were subsequently executed.*
>
> *After having seen comrades who had been mutilated by partisans, we were little shocked by this grim treatment. That's how one was brutalized by the partisan war."*

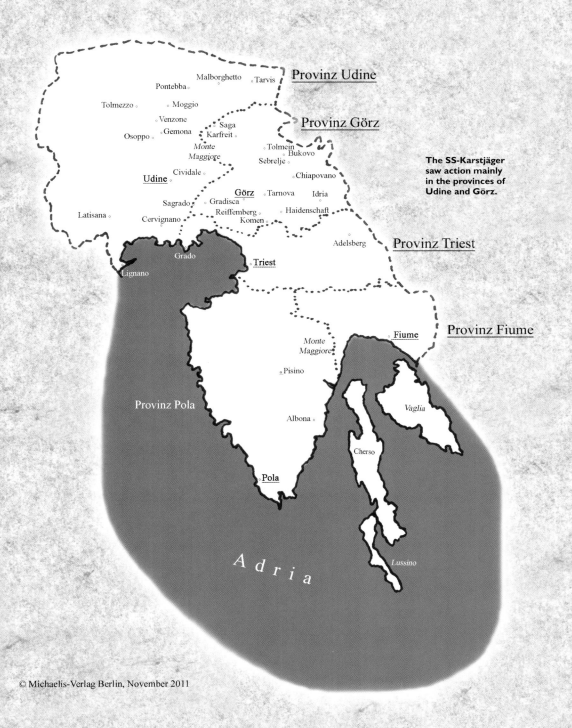

Provinz Udine

Provinz Görz

The **SS-Karstjäger** saw action mainly in the provinces of Udine and Görz.

Provinz Triest

Provinz Fiume

Remnants of the war.
Armored traincars of the
Supreme Commissioner
Adriatic Coastland.

The SS-Karstjäger's area of operations:
Tarvis-Camporosso-Malborghetto-Pontebba.

In September 1943 the SS-Karstwehr-Bataillon was issued two Italian 75mm guns. Like the 65mm mountain cannon, because of its wooden wheels it was not considered for the motorized platoons. Nevertheless, in the photo above an Italian Fiat Spa TL 37 is seen towing the gun. Many Italian volunteers served in the Artillery Battalion until the end of the war.

During the disarming of the Italian Army, the SS-Karstwehr-Bataillon took possession of four Italian 65mm mountain cannon.

SS-Karstjäger in karst and wooded areas.

The pay book of Farnz Löw, an ethnic German from Romania.

A. Zuletzt zuständige Wehrersatzdienststelle:
SS-Erg. Stelle Süd-Ost Wien.

B. Zum Feldheer abgesandt von:¹)

	Ersatztruppenteil	Kompanie	Nr. der Truppen-stammrolle
a	SS-Gren.-Erf.-Btl. „Ost" **Stammkp.**		
b			
c			

C.

	Feldtruppenteil²)	Kompanie	Nr. der Kriegs-stammrolle
a		3.	140
	SS-Karstwehrbataillon	1.	Kr. 244
c			

D.

	Jetzt zuständiger Ersatztruppenteil²)	Standort
	SS-Gren.-Erf.-Btl. „Ost"	**Breslau**
	SS-Karstwehr Ers. Komp. Rottenstein (Oberfr.)	

(Meldung dortselbst nach Rückkehr vom Feldheer oder Lazarett, zuständig für Ersatz an Bekleidung und Ausrüstung)

¹) Vom Ersatztruppenteil einzutragen, von dem der Soldbuchinhaber zum Feldheer abgesandt wird.
²) Vom Feldtruppenteil einzutragen und bei Versetzungen von einem zum anderen Feldtruppenteil derart abzuändern, daß die alten Angaben nur durchstrichen werden, also leserlich bleiben.

Weiterer Raum für Eintragungen auf Seite 26

4

Anschriften der nächsten lebenden Angehörigen

des   Franz Löw.
(Vor- und Zuname)

1. Ehefrau: Vor- und Mädchenname

(ggf. Vermerk „ledig")

Wohnort (Kreis)
Straße, Haus-Nr.

2. Eltern: des Vaters, Vor- und Zuname

Josef Löw

Stand oder Gewerbe
der Mutter, Vor- u. Mädchenname

Wohnort (Kreis)   Koppod Nr. 338
Straße, Haus-Nr.   Kreis: Hermannstadt / Rum.

3. Verwandte oder Braut:*)

Vor- und Zuname
Stand oder Gewerbe
Wohnort (Kreis)
Straße, Haus-Nr.

*) Ausfüllung nur, wenn weder 1. noch 2. ausgefüllt sind.

5

In das Lazarett mitgegeben:
Geld, geldwerthabende Papiere, Wertgegenstände u. dergl.

1. Dez. 1943

i. A. SS-Ostuf. u. Kp.führer

Führergeschenk (Sonderlebensmittelkarte, und RM 10'— ausgegeben

am   LEA Wien

Führergeschenk erhalten
O.U. 22. 1. 1944

SS-Obersturmführer u. Kp. Führer

22

In das Lazarett mitgegeben:
Geld, geldwerthabende Papiere, Wertgegenstände u. dergl.

Waffen-SS

O.U., den 10.12.43

SS-Obersturmführer
und Kp. Führer

Klagenfurt, den 3.1.45

Reservelazarett III a Klagenfurt
Schülerheim

23

Löw volunteered in Romania in 1943 and from that summer served in the SS-Karstwehr-Bataillon.

SS-Standartenführer Dr. Hans Brand commanded the SS-Karstwehr-Bataillon from its formation until 23 March 1944.

Photo left: SS-Standartenführer Dr. Brand with SS-Untersturmführer Kühbandner in Pottenstein.

Photo below: SS-Standartenführer Dr. Brand with his adjutant, SS-Obersturmführer Weiland, in the operations zone in the spring of 1944.

Officers and non-commissioned officers of the SS-Karstwehr-Bataillon, end of March 1944.
Sitting, from l. to r.: SS-Obersturmführer Kühbandner, SS-Obersturmführer Weiland, Hauptmann
Bischetsrieder, SS-Standartenführer Dr. Brand, SS-Hauptsturmführer Berschneider, SS-
Hauptsturmführer Ullm and SS-Untersturmführer Vogel.

Officers of the SS-Karstwehr-Bataillon at a German-Italian soccer match in Gradisca.

Photo above from l. to r.: Friedrich Rainer, Supreme Commissioner for the Operations Zone Adriatic Coastland, SS-Standartenführer Dr. Brand, and SS-Gruppenführer Globocnik, Senior SS and Police Commander Adriatic Coastland.

A reserved SS-Standartenführer Dr. Brand accepts thanks from SS-Gruppenführer Globocnik.

Because of the discrepancies with SS-Gruppenführer Globocnik, on 23 March 1944 Himmler placed Dr. Brand in charge of the cave research facility in the karst. The formal farewell took place in Gradisca d'Isonzo on 13 May 1944. Photo below from l. to r.: SS-Gruppenführer Globocnik, Dr. Brand, Gauleiter Rainer.

SS-Gruppenführer Globocnik, Senior SS and Police Commander Adriatic Coastland, delivers a speech.

Following the action in Istria, on 20 April 1944 the SS-Karstwehr-Bataillon took part in the celebration of Hitler's birthday in front of the law courts in Trieste.

The leader of the SS-Karstwehr-Bataillon, SS-Hauptsturmführer Berschneider.

The battalion, marching in and in formation for the Senior SS and Police Commander's speech.

The *24. Waffen-Gebirgs[Karstjäger]-Division der SS*

Formation

Although conscription was introduced in the "Adriatic Coastland" area of operations in autumn 1943, because of feared strikes and revolts the 1923 to 1925 age classes were not mustered until March 1944. In 1944, the 1914 to 1922 plus 1926 age classes were called up. With these personnel from the Adriatic Coastland, Himmler planned to form a *Waffen-Gebirgs[Karstjäger]-Division der SS*.[17] The unit was designated a *Waffen-Division der SS* because the new draftees did not meet the racial requirements of the *Waffen-SS*. The formulation that the men were "members of the Adriatic coastland" was based on the fact that, from an ethnic point of view, they were not a homogenous nationality but included, at least, Italians, Slovenians and Croats.

The approximately 1,000-man-strong *SS-Karstwehr-Bataillon* formed the core of the division. *SS-Sturmbannführer* Hahn, the former commander of *SS-Gebirgsjäger-Ausbildungs- und Ersatz-Bataillon 6* in Hallein, was named to head the formation staff. His task was to form the unit with the following organization:

Division Headquarters	Military Postal Code, 40 731
Waffen-Gebirgs[Karstjäger]-Regiment der SS 59	Military Postal Code, 40 731
I Battalion	Military Postal Code, 05 219
II Battalion	Military Postal Code, 28 657
III Battalion	Military Postal Code, 33 627
Waffen-Gebirgs[Karstjäger]-Regiment der SS 60	
I Battalion	
II Battalion	
III Battalion	
Waffen-Gebirgs-Artillerie-Regiment der SS 24	Military Postal Code, 22 224
I Battalion	
II Battalion	
III Battalion	
SS-Gebirgs-Aufklärungs-Abteilung 24	
SS-Gebirgs-Panzerjäger-Abteilung 24	
SS-Gebirgs-Pionier-Bataillon 24	Military Postal Code, 28 007
SS-Gebirgs-Feldersatz-Bataillon 24	
SS-Gebirgs-Sanitäts-Abteilung 24	Military Postal Code, 32 137
SS-Gebirgs-Veterinär-Kompanie 24	Military Postal Code, 67 130
SS-Gebirgs-Nachrichten-Abteilung 24	Military Postal Code, 34 445
SS-Gebirgs-Ersatz-Kompanie 24	Military Postal Code, 76 728
Kommandeur der SS-Divisions-Nachschubtruppen 24	Military Postal Code, 26 670
SS-Feldpostamt 24	Military Postal Code 43 480
SS-Wirtschafts-Bataillon 24	

---

[17] SS-FHA, Org.Tgb.Nr.2045/44.

The *SS-Führungsshauptamt*'s plans could not be realized, however. Although an age class in the Adriatic Coastland comprised 10,000 men, because of the existing circumstances no significant conscription could be undertaken. Altogether, thirteen age classes were supposed to be mustered in the Adriatic Coastland by the summer of 1943, but as the attitude of the population ranged from basically negative to hostile, recruiting had to be abandoned. As a result, initially only about 400 men were procured for the new division.

When it became apparent that not enough personnel would be coming from the Adriatic Coastland, about 500 South Tyroleans were brought in from the Uggowitza and Malborghetto training camps. These men had been conscripted into the *Ordnungspolizei* in Sterzing and Schlanders in the Alpine Foothills zone of operations in April and May 1944 and were now transferred to the *Waffen-SS*.

Although the new units were to be formed in the Aupa-Pontebba-Malborghetto-Moggio Udinese area, which bordered the Reich, the new division's formation staff remained at the former location of the *SS-Karstwehr-Bataillon*'s headquarters in Gradisca. The same was true of the various platoons and companies, which remained in their garrisons, while others were ordered into the area around Tolmezzo for the formation of new units. The former *SS-Obersturmführer* Hesselbarth remembered:

> *"Then, in June 1944, another group with four companies of South Tyrolean recruits was formed in the SS training camp in Uggowitz, initially with only loose contact with the SS-Karstwehr-Bataillon. I took over one of these companies. Soon afterwards, the SS-Karstwehr-Bataillon and the training camp were combined to create the foundation of the 24. Waffen-Gebirgs[Karstjäger]-Division der SS. Commander of the formation staff was SS-Sturmbannführer Hahn with Weiland as his operations officer. SS-Sturmbannführer Berschneider took over the I Battalion, SS-Obersturmführer Merwald and later SS-Obersturmführer Schluge the II Battalion. As division units, this rump division also had a headquarters company, a cavalry platoon and an armored company."*

As explained here, due to lack of personnel only the following units could be formed:

Formation Staff	Military Postal Code, 40 731
Signals Platoon	Military Postal Code, 34 445
Cavalry Platoon	
Pioneer Platoon	Military Postal Code, 28 007
Waffen-Gebirgs[Karstjäger]-Regiment der SS 1[18]	Military Postal Code, 57 542
Headquarters Company	Military Postal Code, 57 542 A
Anti-Tank Platoon	Military Postal Code, 57 542 B
Infantry Gun Platoon	Military Postal Code, 57 542 C
I Battalion	Military Postal Code, 05 219
Headquarters Company	Military Postal Code, 57 542
II Battalion	Military Postal Code, 28 657
III Battalion	Military Postal Code, 33 627

---

[18] Initially designated with the number 1, it was later renamed Waffen-Gebirgs[Karstjäger]-Regiment der SS 59.

Waffen-Gebirgs[Karstjäger]-Artillerie-Regiment der SS

Gebirgsartillerie-Batterie	Military Postal Code, 22 224
1 armored company	Military Postal Code, 64 584
1 medical company	Military Postal Code, 32 137
1 veterinary company	Military Postal Code, 67 130
1 supply unit	Military Postal Code, 26 760
1 replacement company	Military Postal Code, 67 728
1 field post office	Military Postal Code, 43 480

The former *SS-Sturmmann* Erwin Röslen explained his role in the formation of the II Battalion, *Waffen-Gebirgs[Karstjäger]-Regiment der SS 1*:

> *"Shortly before mid-1944, we learned that our former SS-Karstwehr-Bataillon was being enlarged to form the SS-Karstjäger-Division. The towns of Uggowitza, Malborghetto, Pontebba and Moggia were selected as training sites and Resia for the high mountain company. Instructors were provided by the former battalion.*
>
> *I myself went to Malborghetto, where machinegunners and mortar men were trained, and took over a group of South Tyroleans. Most were the sons of mountain farmers, and they became loyal comrades with whom we stayed in touch even after the war.*
>
> *After the conclusion of training we were transferred to Udine. It was initially planned to form three battalions, which together would have had the approximate strength of a regiment. But this remained no more than a plan. For a time I was tasked with training Italian recruits and tried to make soldiers of them. In vain! Only a few went into action with us in 1945. Little by little, most disappeared.*
>
> *During formation of the II Battalion, elements of the I Battalion were divided into hunting teams and saw action, particularly in the Tolmezzo area."*

As mentioned above, elements of the *SS-Karstwehr-Bataillon* – mainly the 2nd Company – were divided into hunting teams and committed in the large partisan area around Tolmezzo. The later *SS-Unterscharführer* Ludwig Brummer remembered:

> *"In the summer of 1944 we were deployed in hunting teams. The teams were three to six men strong and some of the time we wore civilian clothes. Some of the actions lasted fourteen days and we were always on our own."*

The OKW had issued "Guidelines for Hunting Teams" at the end of August 1942. These were composed like an army manual:

> *"1. To prevent betrayal or premature warning of the enemy, hunting teams shall march into the assigned area at night. By day they shall disappear into woods away from the villages, so that inhabitants will not notice them or their sentries.*
>
> *2. On arriving in the area of operations, the hunting team shall behave exactly like the enemy bandits themselves, specifically:*

a) After carefully scouting the terrain, traps shall be laid for the enemy wherever he may be expected to appear; for example, on roads where the enemy is known to lay mines, on wooden bridges he has repeatedly tried to burn down, or at the edge of forests, close to a village which information from residents suggest is being used as a food supply base for the bandits.

b) The hunting team shall destroy every enemy who walks into the trap. Vastly superior enemy forces are not to be engaged. In this case, report immediately to superior authorities to initiate a larger operation. The hunting team shall remain in contact with the enemy until the arrival of additional forces.

c) A set trap is only successful if the hunting team has great patience. Under some circumstances it must hold out in the same place for several days and nights.

d) If the element of surprise is lost, for example as a result of the chance appearance of residents, the selected location shall be abandoned at once if the troublesome witnesses cannot be eliminated quietly.

e) Likewise, after a successful ambush, the hunting team must leave the area immediately and move to another area to begin a new mission.

3. If possible, hunting teams shall be equipped with radio. Relay stations may have to be established over greater distances.

4. This style of fighting must never be rushed and requires much time.

5. While in the field, the hunting team must be independent of field kitchens or requisitions.

It must therefore take with it a carefully-planned store of field rations for at least fourteen days. These rations shall consist of tinned meat, chocolate, tobacco products, bread, and coffee or tea.

6. After the successful completion of an operation, the hunting team shall occupy rest quarters. During this time the men shall be well fed and given priority in the allocation of market goods.

7. The hunting team must undergo retraining before departing on a new mission, in particular live firing with machineguns and sub-machineguns and throwing of live grenades. Through constant target shooting, machinegunners and sub machinegunners, in particular, must learn to fire accurately while walking or running.

8. Winter exercises shall begin as soon as the first snow falls.

9. All relevant experiences and reconnaissance results shall be forwarded to the hunting teams by the fastest means.

10. Membership in a hunting team is a distinction."

In addition to about 500 South Tyroleans and about 400 members of the Adriatic Coastland, by 20 September 1944, the unit was also assigned an additional 100 ethnic and Reich Germans, resulting in the following strengths:

	Officers	**NCOs**	**Enlisted Men**	**Total**
Actual	27	163	1,799	1,989
	1.4%	8.2%	90.4%	100%
Authorized	165	898	5,563	6,626
	2.4%	13.6%	84%	100%

The men from the Adriatic Coastland initially formed the III Battalion. Leonhard L., a former Italian member of the division, remembered:

> *"I was born in the province of Görz in 1927 and in April 1944 had to complete my compulsory labor service in the Todt Organization. Few of us young lads had much enthusiasm for this. I was employed in Görz and the surrounding area building roads, and after about half a year I was released from service. Soon afterwards I was drafted by the Waffen-SS and was immediately sent to join the III Battalion of the Waffen-Gebirgs[Karstjäger]-Regiment der SS 1 in Gradisca. My instructors were ethnic Germans from Romania. Fortunately everything was delayed and so I did not take part in any actions with the unit."*

After it had been demonstrated that tanks could play a not to be underestimated role in anti-partisan warfare, a panzer company was formed for the new *24. Waffen-Gebirgs[Karstjäger]-Division der SS* in Cividale (approx. twenty km east of Udine). It was issued several examples of the Italian P40 heavy tank. At the end of September 1944 the division, which was in the midst of the formation process, had:

11	Italian P 40 tanks
6	75-mm mountain guns
4	45-mm infantry guns
24	81.4-mm mortars
20	heavy machineguns
75	light machineguns
150	pistols
150	sub-machineguns
1,250	rifles

The unit was obviously under-armed, given its personnel strength.

At the same time, the SS-*Karstwehr-Ersatz-Kompanie* was moved from Pottenstein, initially to Gradisca for about four weeks and then to Cividale. This enabled strength in the area of operations to be increased, at least nominally.

In Tolmezzo at the end of September 1944, the first examples of the Anti-Partisan War Badge in Bronze and Silver, instituted in February of that year, were presented to members of the *SS-Karstwehr-Bataillon*.

Following the reorganization into two and then three battalions, there was a resumption in major operations after partisans proclaimed the *Zona Libera della Carnia e del Friuli* (Free Zone of Carnia and Friaul) in Ampezzo (approx. twenty km west of Tolmezzo) on 26 September 1944. Units of the *Waffen-Gebirgs[Karstjäger]-Regiment der SS 1* took part in "Operation Klagenfurt" until 30 September. The operation, which involved units of the *Wehrmacht*, *Waffen-SS* and *Ordnungspolizei*, was not a success, however. It was followed by "Operation *Waldläufer*" (ranger) in the same area from the 8th to the 22nd of October. Elements of the *Waffen-Gebirgs[Karstjäger]-Regiment der SS 1* were committed between Tolmezzo and the border of the German Reich, together with units of the 10th and 15th SS Police Regiments and the 71st Infantry Regiment. The award application for the German Cross in Gold for *SS-Gruppenführer* Globocnik, the

Senior SS and Police Commander Adriatic Coastland, dated 25 February 1945 contains information about the two operations:

> *"In "Operation Klagenfurt," by virtue of his skilled use of forces and constant presence, he succeeded in destroying the bandits despite the constantly changing enemy situation in this area. Serious crises were overcome through the flexible deployment of his forces, ultimately resulting in losses to the enemy of 500 killed.*
>
> *During the second week of operations against the bandits, in addition to other operations, "Operation Waldläufer," in particular, was a complete success. Although command faced extremely difficult situations, here too he so mauled the bandits that they were unable to maintain larger units. The enemy left 105 dead on the battlefield, while our own losses were minimal. 165 prisoners were taken. Two German officers and seventy-one NCOs and men of the German Police were freed from bandit captivity. Much booty was taken.*
>
> *For the operations carried out by SS-Gruppenführer Globocnik in the province of Udine, which demanded extraordinary performances by commanders and troops, in addition to a personal telex in the Honor Roll of the Reichsführer-SS, the Reichsführer-SS has announced that:*
>
> *In the month of October 1944, SS and police units under the command of SS-Gruppenführer und Generalleutnant der Polizei Globocnik distinguished themselves through conspicuous bravery and steadfastness in the fighting against Tito groups east of Udine. I have expressed my appreciation to prominent units and individual fighters."*

In autumn 1944, the *24. Waffen-Gebirgs[Karstjäger]-Division der SS* received additional reinforcements, 300 men from the Adriatic Coastland and about 170 Spanish volunteers. Some of the latter were former members of the 250th (Spanish) Infantry Division, which had been formed for the battle against the Soviet Union and then disbanded in the summer of 1943. The later *SS-Unterscharführer* Wilfried Sonnenwald described them:

> *"I remember the Spaniards very well. They didn't fight, as they had originally volunteered for the Eastern Front. I can still see them riding around in Tolmezzo with open umbrellas on bicycles they had 'organized.'"*

Former *SS-Sturmmann* Holluschek described the complexity of the SS unit:

> *"With us were Reich Germans, ethnic Germans from the Banat, Transylvania and the Soviet Union, Slovenes and Croats, Bosnians and even Spaniards from the disbanded Blue Division. The latter refused to fight, however, as they only wanted to fight against Bolshevism and not against the English in the Balkans. To get along in this group one had to have good knowledge of several languages. Of course the Italians can also not be forgotten.*

We had a little Croat with us who never washed. We said to him: Come on, wash yourself! No, he answered, water no good, too cold. And so we washed him. He cried every time – our handling wasn't very gentle. What no one could believe though, was that he didn't desert and stayed with us to the end.

Many foreign volunteers had tears in their eyes on 8 May 1945 and we had to "send some back" – they actually wanted to remain with us."

On 27 November 1944 the Commander of the *Waffen-SS* "Italy" reported the strength of the *24. Waffen-Gebirgs[Karstjäger]-Division der SS* as:

	Officers	NCOs	Enlisted Men	Total
Actual	42	258	2,179	2,479
	1.4%	8.2%	90.4%	100%
Authorized	165	898	5,563	6,626
	2.4%	13.6%	84%	100%

The breakdown of personnel was roughly as follows:

Reich Germans	750 men
Ethnic Germans	850 men
Residents of the Adriatic Coastland	700 men
Spaniards	170 men

"Operation *Achse*" (axis) began the same day that this report was written. Once again under the command of *SS-Gruppenführer* Globocnik, the goal of the operation was to clear partisans from an area of planned defensive position against the advancing British.[19] Elements of the *SS-Karstjäger* in Udine were also moved to Tolmezzo. The operation ended on 13 December 1944, and it was claimed that 206 partisans had been killed and another 120 wounded.

This was followed by "Operation *Adler*" (Eagle) in the Görz-Haidenschaft area from the 19th to 25th of December 1944. The following is from the previously cited award application for the German Cross in Gold for *SS-Gruppenführer* Globocnik:

"Operation Adler deprived the bandits of their entire supply base, drove them back into the inhospitable hills and also inflicted significant losses on them. The bandits lost 488 killed, 123 wounded and large quantities of war materiel."

---

[19] As early as late September 1944, planning began for the construction of stronger defensive positions on the line Tolmein-Isonzo-north of Görz-Farnowones-Birnbaumer Baum-Adelsberger Pforte-Save.

In front of the quarters in Gradisca.

Members of the signals platoon.

SS-Karstjäger in action.

On the way to the operations zone, checking the population, and the aftermath of combat.

If an action was further away from their base, when practicable the **SS-Karstjäger** were transported to the vicinity of the combat area by train.

From there the men proceeded with their pack animals or entirely on foot.

Sergio Corbatti

Trnova

Idrija

Lokve

Haidenschaft

Gate to the battalion compound in Tolmezzo.

The Karfreit area.

The Isonzo River.

Gradisca.

SS-Karstjäger: right, SS-Obersturmführer Weiland beside an Italian-made tank damaged by partisans.

SS-Obersturmführer Weiland, the battalion adjutant.

Tommaso Chiussi

Sergio Corbatti

The **SS-Karstjäger** frequently operated with civilians or as civilians. Above: Slovenian farmers lead a group of **SS-Karstjäger** through the wintry landscape. Below: In the summer of 1942 hunting teams were formed, in particular by the 2nd Company, for operations in the Tolmezzo area.

The Unit is Renamed the *Waffen-Gebirgs[Karstjäger]-Brigade der SS*

After it became clear that the number of men raised in the Adriatic Coastland was far short of what was required to raise the former *SS-Karstwehr-Bataillon* to division strength, on 5 December 1944 the unit was reduced to a *Waffen-Gebirgs[Karstjäger]- Brigade der SS*. The completion of formation through reintegration of the division was to be reported by 30 January 1945.[20]

As no additional personnel were received, the unit's organization remained unchanged:

Formation Staff	*SS-Sturmbannführer* Hahn
Signals Platoon	*SS-Sturmscharführer* Farensky
Cavalry Platoon	*Waffen-Obersturmführer* Borsatti
Pioneer Platoon	*SS-Hauptscharführer* Trautmannsberg
Anti-Tank Platoon	*SS-Oberscharführer* Stähle

Waffen-Gebirgs[Karstjäger]-Regiment der SS 59

I Battalion	*SS-Sturmbannführer* Berschneider
II Battalion	*SS-Obersturmführer* Merwald
III Battalion	*SS-Obersturmführer* Kühbandner[21]

Waffen-Gebirgs[Karstjäger]-Artillerie-Regiment der SS 24

Gebirgsartillerie-Batterie	*SS-Untersturmführer* Wüst
Panzer Company	*SS-Obersturmführer* Behrend
Medical Company	*SS-Hauptsturmführer* Dr. Habisreutinger
Supply Company	*SS-Hauptsturmführer* Ullm
Replacement Company	*SS-Untersturmführer* Bender

It also proved impossible to report the formation of the brigade as completed by 30 January 1945. Instead there were signs of growing unreliability, especially among the Italian members, and soon afterwards orders were issued for the disbandment of the III Battalion, *Waffen-Gebirgs[Karstjäger]-Regiment der SS 59*.

A second wave of decorations with the Anti-Partisan War Badge in Bronze and Silver to members of the *Waffen-Gebirgs[Karstjäger]-Brigade der SS* followed on 30 January 1945.

---

[20] SS-FHA, Org.Tgb.Nr.4694/44.
[21] SS-Obersturmführer Kühbandner was named to command the III Battalion. Since 1943 he had from time to time served as commander of the combined 2nd and 4th Companies of the SS-Karstwehr-Bataillon.

Combat Operations 1945

In January 1945 the II Battalion of *Waffen-Gebirgs[Karstjäger]-Regiment der SS 59* was moved into the Grado-Lignano area, some ninety kilometers to the south. While the South Tyrolean recruits had taken part in a variety of actions – for example guarding the Cereschiatis Passes between Moggio Udinese and Pontebba – the leadership now wanted to send them into direct action against the partisans. Positions were to be expanded and manned in the area of the Marano Lagoon to meet a potential landing by the Allies. Then *SS-Sturmmann* Erwin Röslen remembered:

> *"From our previous area of operations, we were transferred by foot in the direction of the Adriatic. I think it was the Latisana area. It was said that a landing from the sea was expected there. We dug tank defense holes and machinegun positions. The male population was forced to assist us. Each day there were fewer, and so, on orders from SS-Untersturmführer Newton, one Sunday I had to bring the mayor of the surrounding town to him. I set off on my bicycle to find the gentleman. I finally found him after searching in various places. But he didn't want to come with me, claiming he had no bicycle, that he was sick, etc. I assured him that I would return him. Meanwhile a large number of townspeople had gathered and their mood towards me was threatening. I had no choice but to use my carbine to take a bicycle from a young Italian so that the mayor could be made mobile. I felt much better when we had left the town behind us. After some time we were moved right up to the Adriatic, with the exception of the train. We made the move by night, for by day the sky was filled with fighter-bombers and Lightnings. We landed in a small city with a fishing port. From there we went to a house right on the water. Prepared plank beds and emergency rations were waiting for us. Not long afterward, cases of malaria developed. Clouds of flies filled the air in the late evening. I also got sick. The medic gave me a handful of quinine. He told me that he couldn't send me back to the hospital. After several days of high fever I was alright again.*
>
> *Our forces to meet a landing from the sea – especially heavy weapons – were so meager that our resistance would have been trifling. The only artillery we saw in the area was a battery of long-barreled 105mm guns. There were only tractors for two guns.*
>
> *By day the enemy also controlled the air over the entire area."*

The *Waffen-Gebirgs[Karstjäger]-Brigade der SS* was spread out over an area about ninety kilometers long and sixty wide. The I Battalion was in the Udine area and the Replacement Company and the SS Panzer Company in Gradisca. Because of problems finding personnel, the III Battalion had been disbanded in the quartering area in Tolmezzo in spring 1945 and its core personnel had been transferred, mainly to the II Battalion. The Spanish volunteers formed the 5th Company. The 12th Company was merged with the 8th Company. Most of the remaining foreign volunteers were sent to the train to serve as pack animal drivers. The only unit which to a certain extent continued to be made up of Italians was the Mountain Artillery Battery.

In contrast to I Battalion, which consisted almost exclusively of members of the former *SS-Karstwehr-Bataillon*, in II Battalion new collar patches were issued in the spring of 1945. Like all collar patches for (foreign) *Waffen* units of the SS, they had their own symbols. Then *SS-Rottenführer* Otto Walther remembered:

> "In February 1945, we were in the area east of Venice, we had to remove the SS collar patches from our uniforms and sew on new ones bearing a karst thistle. Although the rank badges remained the same, at the time we saw it as a demotion. No one liked that!"

At the same time, in order to deceive the enemy, on 10 February 1945 the brigade was again renamed a division. Although no additional personnel were received, henceforth the unit's official designation was again the *24. Waffen-Gebirgs[Karstjäger]-Division der SS* .[22]

The I Battalion took part in "Operation *Frühlingsanfang*" (First Day of Spring), which began on 20 March 1945. The operation was commanded by *SS-Standartenführer* Ludolf von Alvensleben, the Senior SS and Police Commander Adriatic West (previously designated Senior SS and Police Commander Udine). It was carried out in the area north of the Idrijca River in the Tarnow Forest and also involved elements of the 1st SS Cossack Cavalry Division. The operation was completed on 6 April 1945. Then *SS-Oberscharführer* Franz Ludwig remembered:

> "We first encountered the Cossacks during operations in the Trnova Forest. They went into action with women, who served as assistant medics. With its large, almost primeval forest, the area of operations was particularly treacherous and demanded everything of us. We succeeded in encircling the partisan nests in Trnova and Lokve, which had been identified during previous operations, and crushed not inconsiderable partisan units. We found that the few wells in the area, where there were no civilians to be seen, had been poisoned with the bodies of animals. There was a dead donkey in a well from which we drew water, but we failed to see it in the darkness. We drank the water – thank God no one got sick – and then the next morning we discovered the "fine mess."
>
> We found that a growing number of partisans were infiltrating into the area of operations. Despite our best intentions, with our weak armament we were unable to prevent it. We occupied the area, but only in small groups manning scattered strongpoints.
>
> We were told that the partisans were massing to provide a base for Allied airborne troops in the event that the enemy was unable to break through the southern front."

---

[22] Reichsführer-SS, field command office, secret command matter 1698/45 of 10 February 1945.

Three days later the Allies launched their offensive in Italy. On 25 April 1945 the British 8th Army crossed the Po and advanced on Venice and Trieste. This made a hypothetical airborne landing redundant. Then *SS-Unterscharführer* Heinz Frost remembered a final mission in April 1945, still on the Adriatic:

> *"In the spring of 1945, our platoon (1st Platoon, 7th Company) was assigned to defend the coast. As large groups of partisans were up to no good in our rear area, on or about 21 April 1945 our platoon received orders to occupy the nearby small town of Cervinano and defend it against advancing partisan groups. As our platoon approached the small town, we came under heavy fire. Unaware of the strength of the enemy forces in the town, our weak platoon attacked. There was fierce street fighting between us and the partisans. They shot from every window and other holes. All of the doors were locked and we couldn't find any cover. While advancing, my best friend Alt was shot through the lower abdomen. I myself was wounded in both feet by hand grenade fragments. With losses mounting, we were forced to retreat. We wounded were transferred to a naval artillery aide station in the nearest town. At his request, the badly wounded Horst Alt's bed was placed next to mine. I frequently had to comfort him. He laid his head on my chest. When I awoke from a half-sleep at about three in the morning, I noticed that his head was heavy and that he wasn't moving. I immediately called the doctor, who discovered that Horst had bled out and was dead. As the British were not far away, that same day we were loaded into trucks. We took Alt with us, wrapped in a tent square, as his last request had been to be buried in the mountains. For days Horst in his tent square was my companion on one of the train's horse-drawn wagons. As the effort became too great for us, we buried him in a coffin in a small village near Udine."*

On 25 April 1945 the Italian partisans called for a national uprising. Four days later Allied troops reached Venice, which had been evacuated by the Germans the day before. On that 29 April 1945, in Caserta *SS-Obergruppenführer* Wolff, the Supreme SS and Police Commander in Italy, signed the surrender of German forces in Italy. As it called for all German troops to immediately leave Italy, the retreat to the border of the Reich began.

When, at the end of April, partisans blocked the important road through the Tagliamento Valley between Osoppo and Gemona, I Battalion of *Waffen-Gebirgs[Karstjäger]-Regiment der SS 59* was sent from the Udine area to reopen it. Together with the regiment's II Battalion coming from the coast of the Adriatic, it was attached to SS Battle Group Harmel. The battle group's mission was to secure the Osoppo-Gemona-Venzone area. In addition to the SS *Karstjäger*, *SS-Brigadeführer* Harmel had under his command *SS-Gebirgsjäger-Ausbildungs-und-Ersatz- Bataillon 7* and *SS-Polizei-Regiment 10*. SS Battle Group Harmel, approximately 5,000 men strong, was attached to the *XXII. Gebirgs-Korps* under *General der Gebirgstruppen* Lanz. Then *SS-Oberscharführer* Franz Ludwig remembered:

"At the end of April 1945, the Italian partisans blocked the area between Osoppo and Gemona. As almost all of the troops and rear-echelon units were marching north out of the Adriatic zone through the Tagliamento Valley, there was a danger that everything would become backed up there and fall easy prey to Allied aircraft. We therefore received orders to open up the march route. Under constant machinegun and mortar fire from the mountains, we were nevertheless able to force the partisans back somewhat. In the process we were also fired upon from every village."

During the attempt to clear the retreat area, on 2 May 1945 near Avasinis (approx. twelve km west of Gemona) fifty-one civilians were shot.

On 25 April 1945, the II Battalion, *Waffen-Gebirgs[Karstjäger]-Regiment der SS 59* was placed on alert on the Adriatic and initially assembled in San Giorgio de Nagaro. From there, marching by night, at the beginning of May 1945 it reached the positions in the Osoppo-Gemona area and relieved the regiment's I Battalion, which moved further north. A former member remembered the constant battles with partisans:

"In the first days of May 1945 we relieved the I Battalion in Ospedaletto (approx. 4.5 km north of Gemona). A large anti-tank barrier had been placed in front of the town. It was the day after the news that the Führer had fallen in Berlin. We and the entire battalion train were encircled by partisans and spent the whole day under mortar fire."

The former *SS-Sturmmann* Erwin Röslen described the retreat from the Adriatic:

"As I was a messenger in the company headquarters squad and had a bicycle, my company commander, SS-Untersturmführer Newton, made me responsible for keeping our march column together. That was not easy. One night after a halt, I lost contact. I rode back several kilometers and then heard the whinnying of horses and the stamping of hoofs. Thank God, I had found the group again. The drivers of the leading vehicles were asleep on their train wagons with heads hanging, and tank noises could be heard some distance away. The English (New Zealand) troops had to be nearby. As it turned out, however, they veered right in the direction of Trieste and at first left us alone.

I gave the drivers hell and they were soon awake, then we set off at a good pace to catch up with the rest of the column. During the day we had to conceal ourselves well because of the enemy fighter-bombers.

We marched towards the mountains along the Udine. Heavy rain slowed our progress. After a fighter-bomber attack, we reached Gemona-Osoppo, where anti-tank and mine barriers had already been set up. Then the British tanks caught up with us. There was artillery and tank fire, and the partisans fired at us with machineguns and mortars from the mountainsides. We learned of negotiations between our side and the enemy, who demanded that we leave Italian territory as quickly as possible.

Loyalist Italian officers now also stepped up to the plate. While delivering messages to our battalion command post I encountered such "birds of paradise," who now appeared as victors.

Our defensive operations there ended after about four days and then disengaged at three in the morning. Our vehicles had already been withdrawn. All of the bridges were blown up 100 meters behind us."

As Röslen described, in addition to fighting against partisans there were also engagements with advancing British troops, specifically the 6th New Zealand Armoured Division. On 6-7 May 1945, the last units reached the crest of the Carnish Alps. The II Battalion disbanded there on 9 May 1945, while the II Battalion did likewise about ten kilometers to the east.

Then *SS-Sturmmann* Karl Mörixbauer remembered:

"When the war ended I was in a heavy machinegun position near Venzone. Our retreat took us through Tolmezzo in the direction of Auronzo on the German border, where we then split up into small groups and walked home. We saw no more combat after Tolmezzo."

With the help of his diary, then *SS-Unterscharführer* Wilfried Sonnenwald meticulously described how he became a prisoner of war:

"Our unit was in Tolmezzo until 19 February 1945, when it moved to Pontebba. On 4 March I was at the radio maintenance shop in Moggio. From 16 April on, I was in Porpetto (approx. twenty km west of Gradisca). We left there at about 12:00 on 29 April 1945 and marched to Gonars. By way of Venzone, we arrived in Moggio on 3 May and spent three days there. We left there at about 11:00 and at about 16:00 crossed the Italian border. By bus and truck, we passed Feistritz and Spittal and on 9 May arrived in Zell am See. At about 14:00 the next day we became POWs in a collecting camp in Salzburg. For me this ended on 29 May 1945, when I was handed over to the French."

While many – especially those from South Tyrol – made their way home, some units went into British captivity en masse. This ended operations by the *SS-Karstjäger*. Conceived and trained as a special unit, the war altered its composition and role. Hampered by shortages of officers and non-commissioned officers as well as inadequate equipment, the expansion of the *SS-Karstwehr-Bataillon* into a brigade or division could not be achieved. The question remains, why was the unit not brought up to authorized strength through the addition of larger ethnic German contingents from Croatia, Romania or Hungary or transfers of air force or navy personnel, as was common in other SS formations in 1944-45.

About 100 *Karstjäger* were killed in approximately twenty months of combat operations. If one compares this to formations fighting on the Eastern Front at the same time, it becomes obvious – despite the tragedy of the partisan war – that the *SS-Karstjäger* were deployed in a secondary theater of war.

A cavalry platoon of about thirty-five men was formed in 1944.

Quarters in Udine.

About 100 SS-Karstjäger were killed in action between 9 September 1943 and 9 May 1945.

SS-Gruppenführer Globocnik, Senior SS and Police Commander Adriatic Coastland (4th from right), personally led operations against the partisans on many occasions. Here he received the German Cross in Gold on 7 February 1945. Globocnik, who had previously been tasked with the final solution of the Jewish question in Poland, committed suicide after he, Gauleiter Rainer and others were captured by British troops in a hut on the Möslacher Alm in Carinthia.

The collar patch with the karst thistle, introduced in 1945.

Appendices

Brief Biographies of the Commanders

Josef Berschneider was born in Neumarkt (Oberpfalz) on 29 November 1902. He was a member of the *Allgemeine-SS* and was carried by the *1. SS-Standarte* in Munich until the end of the war. He was promoted to *SS-Untersturmführer* on 9 November 1934, to *SS-Obersturmführer* one year later, and on 11 September 1938 to *SS-Hauptsturmführer*. In 1938 he joined the *SS-Standarte "Deutschland"* (*SS-Verfügungstruppe*) with the rank of *SS-Untersturmführer*. In July 1941, *SS-Obersturmführer* Berschneider took over the 5th Company of *SS-Infanterie-Regiment 6 (mot.)*. Two years later, by then an *SS-Hauptsturmführer*, he was transferred to the *SS-Karstwehr-Bataillon* in Pottenstein. There he commanded the 1st and 3rd Companies for a time. Berschneider was decorated with the Iron Cross, Second Class on 30 October 1943, and, from autumn 1943, he several times served as deputy battalion commander. After March 1944 he was essentially battalion commander. Berschneider was promoted to *SS-Sturmbannführer* on 21 June 1944. As such he commanded the I Battalion of *Waffen-Gebirgs[Karstjäger]-Regiment der SS 59* until the end of the war. The following is from the award application for the Iron Cross, First Class:

> *"Prior to his transfer to Italy, until July 1943 SS-Sturmbannführer Berschneider served as company commander and regimental special duties officer in Karelia and distinguished himself there in attacks on Salla and Sojanna and in the capture of Kiestinki.*
>
> *His first significant action in Upper Italy was the command of a battle group during the disarming of the Italian military in Tarvis. He led the charge that resulted in the collapse of Italian resistance after a short, sharp battle and brought in a general and 800 prisoners. Acting quickly, he occupied the Tarvis railway station and two barracks. On 8 November 1943, his drive and prudent command resulted in the destruction of a bandit battalion on Monte Maggiore near Karfreit. The bandit group was completely destroyed, partly in close combat, and left 210 dead in the forest. Our own losses were minimal. In 1944, while commanding his company and often the entire battalion, SS-Sturmbannführer Berschneider has again shown himself to be a brave and daring commander, especially during Operations "Edelweiss," "Enzian," "Osterglocke," "Braunschweig," "Annemarie" and "Hannelore," in which large bandit forces were destroyed thanks to his command skills and personal bravery.*
>
> *SS-Sturmbannführer Berschneider is a holder of the Iron Cross, Second Class, the Infantry Assault Badge in Silver, the Eastern Medal and the War Merit Cross Second Class with Swords. SS-Sturmbannführer Berschneider has been recommended for the Anti-Partisan War Badge in Silver because of fifty recognized bandit combat days."*

Hans Brand was born in Bayreuth on 9 April 1879 and graduated as a Doctor of Engineering in the field of mountain biology. He served as a *Hauptmann* in the heavy artillery during the First World War and was decorated with the Iron Crosses, First and Second Class. After the war, Dr. Brand taught at the Gisela Secondary School in Munich. In April 1939 he joined the *Das Ahnenerbe* Ancestral Heritage Research and Teaching Society and applied for membership in the SS. He was subsequently taken into the *Reichsführer-SS'* personal staff as an SS officer on September 1939 and was named head of the Research Establishment for the Study of Karsts and Caves. His suggestions resulted in the formation of the *SS-Karstwehr-Kompanie* in July 1942. He commanded the company – which was soon expanded into a battalion – until March 1944. As he was an instructor by training, Brand was released from active military service and placed in charge of the newly established cave research facility in the karst. In fact, Dr. Brand was ill suited to command a formation engaged in unconventional partisan warfare. Then *SS-Sturmmann* Erwin Röslen aptly described Dr. Brand:

"As to the personality of Dr. Brand, I can say that his attitude at that time could be described as conservative. To his young soldiers he was more of a father figure than an absolute military superior. Later he was replaced."

When *SS-Standartenführer* Dr. Brand learned of the formation order for the *Waffen-Gebirgs[Karstjäger]-Division der SS*, he wrote to Himmler that he was very pleased and viewed it as recognition of the special karst unit formed by him. He expressed the hope that he would be named inspector of all existing and future *SS-Karstwehr* formations. He was not satisfied with his current position as head of the cave research facility in the karst and hoped to regain an active military role. Then *SS-Oberscharführer* Franz Ludwig remembered Dr. Brand:

"Brand was a theorist. It was easier to imagine him as a teacher in a high school or giving a slide show than as a commander in the war against the partisans. He had probably been a theorist in the First World War, calculating the flight paths of the artillery, rather than standing in the trenches. He thought that one could reasonably solve the problems with the partisans and he probably felt that he had been called to do so. In fact, in the beginning he met with nationalist Slovenian partisan leaders and told them something to the effect that, unfortunately there was a war on, but that they should still attempt to come to terms with the situation. It would do no one any good if both sides killed each other. There would also be a return to peace. In fact Dr. Brand was not unknown among educated people in the operations zone, as he had researched the local karst mountains in the 1920s. And, as difficult as it is to believe, initially there was agreement among the partisans. Brand then wanted responsibility for the entire anti-partisan effort transferred to him, as he had practically created peaceful tranquility.

If the nationalist Slovenian partisans were not entirely unreceptive, there was just as little agreement with the Slovenian Communists as with all the Italian partisans. When, in 1943, several boys from our SS-Karstwehr-Bataillon were massacred by communist partisans, Brand was visibly shocked. The reality was just something different than what he wished."

Werner Hahn was born in Krischow on 2 October 1901 and he became a career soldier in 1919. After serving in a variety of units, including the *von Brandis Freikorps*, his twelve-year period of service ended in 1931. On 20 October of the same year he joined the *Allgemeine-SS*. In 1934 he was promoted to *SS-Untersturmführer* and in 1935 to *SS-Obersturmführer*, then in 1936 he volunteered for service in the *Wehrmacht* mountain troops. In 1937, Hahn was named *Leutnant der Reserve*. He was awarded the Bar to the Iron Cross, Second Class for his service in the Polish campaign. After the campaign against France, on 5 September 1940 he was awarded the Iron Cross, First Class. On 1 October 1941 on the Eastern Front, he received the Infantry Assault Badge in Silver and in 1942 was named *Oberleutnant der Reserve*. On 21 February 1943, Hahn transferred to the *Waffen-SS* with the rank of *SS-Hauptsturmführer der Reserve*. On 17 April he took over *SS-Gebirgsjäger-Ausbildungs- und Ersatz-Bataillon 6* in Hallein. He was promoted to *SS-Sturmbannführer der Reserve* on 9 November 1943. From 15 August 1944 until the end of the war, Hahn commanded the formation staff of the *24. Waffen-Gebirgs[Karstjäger]-Division der SS* and the *24. Waffen-Gebirgs[Karstjäger]-Brigade der SS*.

The Adriatic Coastland Zone of Operations

Italian war-weariness plus the fact that the majority of the population had had enough of fascism, led to the Duce being deposed by Italian King Victor Emmanuel III on 25 July 1943. Marshall Badoglio was tasked with forming a new government and disbanded the Fascist Party. As new prime minister, on 8 September 1943 he signed a ceasefire with the Allies.

To safeguard the strategically- and economically-important northern zone of Italy, the next day Hitler sent German troops into the area. On 12 September 1943, German paratroops freed Mussolini from house arrest on the Gran Sasso. Eleven days later the Duce proclaimed the Italian Socialist Republic, whose territory initially extended from the German border in the north to the line Salerno-Barletto.

As Hitler was fully aware that Mussolini and the reborn Fascist Party had little support among the population, on 1 October 1943 he had the provinces of South Tyrol, Belluno and Trentino combined into Operations Zone Alpine Foothills. Living there were about 135,000 ethnic Germans as an ethnic minority under Peter Hofer. Franz Hofer, Gauleiter of Tyrol-Vorarlberg, provisionally took over the administration of the territory. At the same time the Operations Zone Adriatic Coastland was formed with the Italian provinces Udine (Friaul), Görz, Trieste, Pola (Istria) and Fiume (Quarnero). Rainer, head of the civil administration and Reich Governor of Carinthia, was installed as High Commissioner.

Although it was part of the territory of the new Italian-Fascist state, both operations zones were under purely German administration. In the area of the Operations Zone Adriatic Coastland, the Senior SS and Police Commander Adriatic Coastland (*SS-Gruppenführer und Generalleutnant der Polizei* Globocnik) was installed with headquarters in Trieste. Under his command were the SS and Police Commanders Udine, Görz, Trieste, Istria and Quarnero.

The province of Udine (Friaul) in the northwest of the newly created Operations Zone Adriatic Coastland was populated largely by Italians, who for the most part called themselves Friulians. The partisans encountered in this area were recruited from them and most were either orientated towards the monarchists or communists. The former called themselves *Italia Libera*, often wore bersaglieri uniforms and were military-oriented. They wanted to fight fascism but were skeptical of the new Badoglio government. Their objectives were an independent Italy and continued dominance of the Adriatic area. Many Italians joined the partisans to avoid being sent to Germany as laborers. After partisan life came to appeal even less to them than potential service in the German armaments industry, groups regularly reported voluntarily to the German authorities. Although they were fighting the same enemy, there were repeated confrontations with the, mainly communist-oriented, groups who called themselves Garibaldi partisans.[23] They frequently acted extremely ruthlessly against their military-oriented opponents as well as internal political enemies.[24] An example of this was the murder of Catholic partisans of the Ossopo Brigade by communist guerillas near Porzus on 7 February 1945. The reason behind the murders was in part the desire of the communists to bring additional areas – in this case the province of Udine – under Tito's control.

The province of Görz, which bordered the province of Udine to the east, was largely settled by Slovenians. Only in the western part of the province was there an Italian minority. The partisans there were almost exclusively Slovenian in origin and most were led by communist-oriented officers. There was no strong nationalist partisan movement, although the often forcibly recruited Slovenians were skeptical of communism. Nevertheless, attacks there were also carried out with the violence communist partisans were known for. Then *SS-Rottenführer* Leonhard Eckstein remembered:

> *"In February 1944 we were suddenly roused from our night rest and force-marched into the karst mountains near Komen. Near a village with the German name Reifenberg, we found the bodies of a police company that had been ambushed. All were dead save one. While driving through a ravine at night, the motorized column had suddenly been attacked by partisans from all sides. They had no chance. The survivors, all wounded, were rounded up, some had their clothes taken, their limbs broken, their sex organs cut off, others their eyes put out. Having rushed to the scene through the karstic terrain, we stood helplessly, tears in our eyes and filled with rage. We were all inwardly marked forever."*

The province of Trieste bordered the province of Görz to the south and was home to the Triestine ethnic minority, who often had both Italian and Slovenian roots, but which in the course of history had severed themselves from both states socially and politically. The main thrust was a free Trieste, independent of east and west. The partisans active in the area were as a rule Slovenian bandits or Tito partisans acting from Croatia. There were only a few Italians among the guerillas.

The provinces of Pola and Fiume extended to the Adriatic in the south and to the Croatian border in the east. The population was mainly Croatian, some of whom were so-called coastal Croatians and some island Croatians. The partisan groups there were often made up of Italian soldiers who had deserted and Croatian Tito partisans. Almost all were under communist influence.

---

[23] The unit was named for Giuseppe Garibaldi. Born in 1807, he was considered a great folk hero who had fought for the freedom and unity of Italy.

[24] In the area of the SS-*Karstjäger* the opposition included the "Natisone" Division with the 156th Garibaldi Brigade "Buozzi" west of Tolmein, the 157th Garibaldi Brigade "Picellei" north of Nimi, the 158th Garibaldi Brigade "Grimsei" north of Görz, and the 20th Garibaldi Briigade "Trieste" in the Tarnow area.

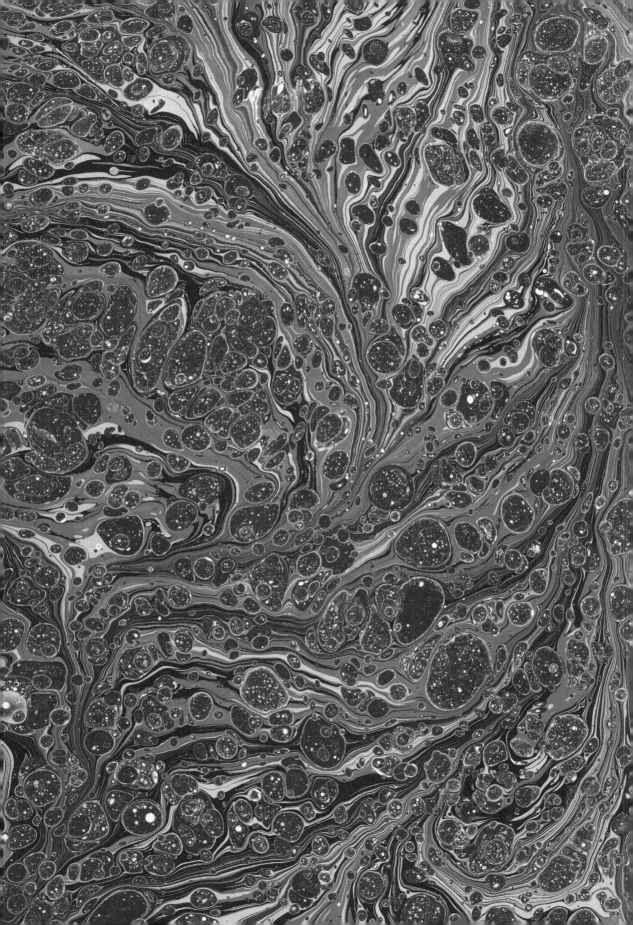